Praise for *Catch Me If*

"I'm happy to be in any club that has Filbert Bayi as a member. You don't have to be a former world record holder to appreciate the determination and commitment he's exemplified to become a legendary runner and someone who graciously gives back to his country."

Sebastian Coe, President, World Athletics; former world record holder at 800m, 1000m, 1500m, and the mile

"The sports world didn't understand Filbert Bayi's racing tactics nor his life experiences when he burst onto the running scene in the '70s. I was very happy to have shared the nuance and technical aspects of hurdling the steeple at a training session in Stockholm along with his coach, Ron Davis. In *Catch Me If You Can*, we see that being a world record holder—just like pursuing a meaningful life—is about courage, discipline, curiosity, and vision. Filbert inspires us all to achieve excellence and impact."

Edwin Moses, 1976 and 1984 Olympic gold medalist, 400m hurdles; former world record holder and winner of 122 consecutive races in the event; Bachelor of Science in physics, Morehouse College

"I never met anybody who trained harder or smarter than Filbert and I am fortunate to be part of his story. His impact on me, the world of running, and our country of Tanzania will last for generations. I'm glad I met Filbert Bayi. When you read *Catch Me If You Can,* you will be too."

Suleiman Nyambui, 1980 Olympic silver medalist, 5000m; former world record holder, indoor 5000m; 1987, 1988 Berlin Marathon winner; 1988 Stockholm Marathon winner

"We should all be thankful for Filbert's courage and contribution in the middle distances in our time. He elevated the possibilities for all of us and awakened the running world to the power and grace of our sport. His contribution is not about winning and losing but about each of us charting our own path and seeking excellence in the process. *Catch Me If You Can* ensures he will not be forgotten and will inspire anybody who reads it."

Rod Dixon, 1972 Olympic bronze medalist, 1500m; World Cross Country bronze medalist, 1973, 1982; 1983 New York City Marathon winner

"Filbert Bayi. The name alone scared the wits out of every middle-distance runner in the world! But he's one of the nicest, most giving people you'll ever meet. From obscurity, he burst onto the scene and shaped the sport's future with his fast, front-running tactics. I always credited Filbert as the one who made me believe that I could run with the world's best. When you read *Catch Me If You Can*, you'll be inspired to be your best, too."

Eamonn Coghlan, former world record holder, indoor mile; 1983 World Championships 5000m gold medalist; three-time Olympian

"In *Catch Me If You Can*, readers will find Filbert Bayi as a man of substance, a loving and caring human being. He is known for his exploits on the track, but more important to me is what he has given back to his country. When I visited his home and school in Tanzania, I saw well-structured buildings, beautiful playing fields for the children, and comfortable classrooms. Through sport and education, he has played the role of ambassador for many years."

Thandi Lujabe-Rankoe, Ambassador, South Africa and African National Congress; author, *A Dream Fulfilled: Memoirs of an African Diplomat* and *Two Nations, One Vision*

"Filbert's legendary performance at the 1974 Commonwealth Games captivated the sporting world. He has been a friend, advocate, and tireless administrator in support of our historic event for decades and represents the excellence the Commonwealth Games have always embodied. *Catch Me If You Can* provides the inside account of his record-breaking day in Christchurch—and an entire life well lived."

Dame Louise Martin, President, Commonwealth Games Federation

"Filbert Bayi raced the way we'd all like to: go out fast, force your competitors deep into the pain zone, and then hold them with a last-lap surge. The rest of us don't actually race this way, because we haven't got the guts. But Bayi did, especially in his epic world record 1500 meters at the 1974 Commonwealth Games. No less an expert than Roger Bannister called it 'the greatest race I've ever seen,' and I agree.

"Reading *Catch Me If You Can*, I was thrilled to relive Bayi's historic race with his insider commentary. Even better: learning more about Bayi's life, and how he trained himself to beat the best. This is a book that will be enjoyed by any running or track fan who appreciates how the back story contributes to the gold medal."

Amby Burfoot, 1968 Boston Marathon winner; author, *The First Ladies of Running* and *Run Forever*

"From racing buses as a teen in Tanzania to setting world records, from Edwin Moses giving him pointers in the hurdles to a New Englander from America guiding him to an Olympic medal, Filbert Bayi's story is riveting. He and his wife started a school to teach academic excellence with seven young children. Today, there are 1,200 students. Achievements like Filbert's make you think about what you can do for society. It's a great read!"

Larry Rawson, four-time Emmy Award-winning track and field commentator

CATCH ME
IF YOU CAN

Revolutionizing My Sport, Breaking World Records, and Creating a Legacy for Tanzania

FILBERT BAYI

WITH MYLES SCHRAG

Foreword by Segun Odegbami

books with *soul* • Flagstaff, AZ

Catch Me If You Can: Revolutionizing My Sport, Breaking World Records, and Creating a Legacy for Tanzania

ISBN: 978-1-7349899-4-6 (paperback)
ISBN: 978-1-7349899-5-3 (e-book)
Library of Congress Control Number: 2022903575

Cover and interior designed by Dariusz Janczewski
Editorial services by Julie Hammonds, Nancy Schrag, and Joe Schrag
Proofreading by Matt Brann
Books printed by Premier Printing, Winnipeg, Manitoba, Canada

Cover photo by Ed Lacey/Popperfoto/Contributor via Getty Images. Filbert Bayi breaks the 1500m world record at the 1974 Commonwealth Games in Christchurch, New Zealand, followed by John Walker (483), Ben Jipcho (obscured), and Rod Dixon (453).

Soulstice Publishing
PO Box 791
Flagstaff, AZ 86002
(928) 814-8943
www.soulsticepublishing.com
connect@soulsticepublishing.com

To my wife... the strongest, smartest, greatest partner and most loving lady a man could ever have.

Contents

FOREWORD

TO THIS DAY, I HAVE NEVER MET FILBERT BAYI IN PERSON. LIKE MANY sports fans from the 1970s and 1980s—and I most definitely was that, as well as an athlete and eventually a diplomat and journalist—I will never forget Filbert Bayi.

In strange ways, there has always been a link of some sort between Filbert and me along the circuit of African sports. We are of the same generation, even as his name and reputation soared to the stratosphere of unprecedented human achievement.

At some epochal moments in sports history, our paths nearly crossed, but fleetingly. Those times are the only authority with which I write these humble lines in tribute to a man who belongs in the company of athletic gods on Mount Olympus.

In 1976, he and I both had Olympic aspirations. Unlike me, however, leading up to the Montreal Games, the prodigious 23-year-old 1500m runner's name was on everyone's lips, the stuff of pure legend. His staggering world-record performances over the previous two years raised expectations sky high.

The whole world took notice, intrigued by the sheer bravado of the young man running dramatic races leading the field from start to finish, without a pacesetter, and defining his place in the annals of athletics. The race was the birth and demonstration of a new middle-distance running style, loaded with a clear statement and challenge to the world: "catch me if you can."

In the two years between 1974 and 1976, he rarely was caught on the track as he imprinted his name and that of his country, Tanzania, on the global map of athletics. He broke two new world records in that period, including a Commonwealth Games record that still stands today, more than four decades later.

What would this young athlete from the hills of Tanzania do in Montreal?

Unlike East African neighbors Kenya, Uganda, and Ethiopia, Tanzania had no production line of world-class, middle- and long-distance runners, no major athletics achievements to boast of until Filbert came along out of the blue to add a page to the narrative.

He was a breath of fresh air when he arrived on the world athletics scene, running with his own unique, graceful, elegant—and above all, fast—style. Extending physical human capacity, setting new limits of endurance and athleticism, expectations ballooned to new heights. The whole continent rooted for him.

Montreal 1976 was to be Filbert Bayi's Olympics. But he never made it there.

I was at the Olympics, an ordinary, unknown football player representing Nigeria. But I was there only briefly. . .just long enough to be a living witness.

Unfortunately, a day to the commencement of the 1976 Games, the governments of 27 African countries, led by Tanzania and Nigeria, decided to pull out their athletes from the Olympics in protest against the International Olympic Committee not banning the New Zealand contingent for its rugby tour of South Africa, a government whose Black citizens were living under apartheid.

Since Tanzania had announced its withdrawal a week earlier, Filbert didn't go to Montreal. The Nigerian team did go, but almost as soon as we arrived the boycott was announced and we were hurried back to the airport. We had an hour to move out of the Olympic Village. Without prior travel arrangements to leave the country, we ended up huddled together like sardines in the departure hall of the airport for hours. For some, it took days to leave.

That was the first mass boycott in Olympic history. The athletes were lambs on the altar of international politics. As noble as the motive and objective were, the boycott came at a high cost to sport. The world was deprived of seeing the ultimate showdown race, a rematch between Filbert and New Zealand's John Walker, along with the other best 1500m runners in the world.

Filbert did not complain.

In the years that followed, I didn't do too badly on the continent playing in a massively popular sport. I was named the Third-Best African player in 1977 and Second-Best African Player in 1980. I was a prominent member of the Shooting Stars International Football Club. Our team from Ibadan, Nigeria, in 1976 became the first to win the Africa Winners Cup.

I was on the national football team of Nigeria that took the gold medal at the ECOWAS Games in 1977 and won the African Cup of Nations in 1980.

Filbert and I came closest to actually meeting each other at the 1978 "African Olympics," as the All-African Games were called. Nigeria took silver in football at the third All-African Games in Algiers, Algeria, in 1978. Filbert, already a global legend mentioned alongside other African runners such as Shambel Abebe Bikila, Kipchoge Hezekiah Keino, and John Akii-Bua, shone like a million stars in winning the 1500m gold medal.

I made sure to watch him in that race.

In 1980, I was again a witness at the Olympic Games in Moscow. The elements had 'selected' a few lucky athletes from the debris of the 1976 Olympics experience, and given us another chance at Olympic glory.

By 1980, Filbert and I were among the lucky athletes from Montreal 1976 who were offered another chance at Olympic glory. Filbert still had fire in his eyes and the stage to go after his dream of a gold medal; my dream was more modest.

Filbert came away with silver, but what was fascinating was another display of his versatility. He got his medal not in his favorite event but in the 3000m steeplechase. This book reveals how that came about.

In the decades since ending our careers as athletes and retiring into the cocoon of other interests, we have embarked on similar ventures. Even here, Filbert, in his characteristic style, is running from the front and taking the lead.

There are too many stories of African athletes experiencing poverty or tragedy and being neglected by their countries after their playing days were over.

Not so, the story of Filbert Bayi. He has an impeccable track record of giving back to his country through sports and education. Although we belong to the same generation, I have followed his journey and taken useful lessons from his unscripted book of life after sport.

Filbert has lived an exemplary life of service. He is a humble patriot and servant, a sports diplomat, a sports administrator, and a sports educator, creating landmarks and establishing institutions that will live after him and sustain the development of African youth through the combination of sport and scholarship.

I do my best to walk a similar path. Like him, I am a sports diplomat (official Sports Ambassador of the Federal Republic of Nigeria), a sports administrator (managed Nigeria's first individual Olympic gold medalist, Chioma Ajunwa), a scholar (published four books and have been writing a weekly syndicated newspaper column for 40 years), a business and media practitioner (a director in Africa's largest daily sports newspaper, owner of a new FM radio and online television station, and presenter/producer of a live weekly TV programme on Africa's largest TV network with 60 million viewers).

In 2004, he was nearly a decade into establishing the Filbert Bayi Nursery, Primary and Secondary Sports Schools in Tanzania—the first such project by any athlete in Africa—to add to his catalogue of incredible contributions to sports. Inspired by his example, I was laying the foundation stone of the Segun Odegbami International College and Sports Academy (SOCA), an institution in Nigeria that has fed the American collegiate sports system with more than 60 Nigerian athletes on full scholarships in the past 10 years.

SOCA's mission is to provide gifted African children with the twin opportunities of intensive sports training and a solid grounding in education as keys to success in life.

Filbert is a source of inspiration to many of us athletes in Africa, with his pioneering works and outstanding on-going contributions in the fields of youth empowerment and sports development in Tanzania and beyond.

He continues to set the pace for other African sporting greats to follow, blazing the trail for the next generation of athletes.

My first time to speak directly with him finally came in 2021. Through a mutual friend, Ron Davis, who coached Filbert in Moscow and has been a successful mentor for many runners across Africa, it happened. I invited Filbert to join me for the weekly Pan-African television show that I present to a growing audience of viewers across the continent.

A few minutes before the show started, we connected via Zoom.

"Hi, Filbert," I said, as the familiar face of one of the greatest athletes in African history loomed on my computer screen.

"Hello, Segun," the legend replied.

From opposite sides of Africa, the voice and smile were unmistakable. Our chat of a few minutes vaporised time and bridged the distance between us that night. Our conversation took off without missing a beat, like long-lost friends finding each other again.

The conversation was a pleasure, as was accepting the honour of writing the introduction to this great man's book.

I spent seemingly a lifetime waiting for the opportunity to meet Filbert. Now it's your chance—and he's made it much easier to catch him by writing this autobiography.

Filbert's athletic exploits are rooted in a specific time and specific places, including Christchurch, Algiers, Moscow, and other destinations you will read about in the book. But his values and his legacy are timeless. Taken together, all of this is why Filbert Bayi should not be forgotten.

That's Filbert–humble pilgrim, singular athlete, pride of Africa, and a god of the track.

Filbert's story is of an ordinary African who did extraordinary things with tenacity, determination, and intelligence. He succeeded against incredible odds at a time when the world was not designed for an African to achieve. Filbert is a model of that struggle and perseverance.

His life should educate and inspire a new generation of youth in Africa and around the world, illuminating the difficulties, challenges, and prospects so they can drink from the fountain of the experiences and examples he set.

Perhaps they will hear Filbert whispering in their ears, daring them also to…"catch me if you can."

Ambassador Olusegun Odegbami
Member of the Order of the Niger (MON)
Fellow at the Nigerian Institute of Management (FNIM)
Associate Fellow of the Nigerian Institute of International Affairs (AFNIIA)
1980 Olympian

Lagos, Nigeria
March 29, 2022

PREFACE

I HELD WORLD RECORDS IN THE MILE AND 1500-METER RUNS. No matter what else I have done or still will do in my life, those facts will lead the obituaries that are written when I die. Maybe they'll even be on my tombstone.

That's fine with me. In a world of billions of people, where the moments pass by quickly and most are soon-forgotten memories, I'll be happy to have done something positive that is remembered at all.

I have a question for you: do you know me?

There are fans of athletics and running, historians, and people my age who do. As the first Black man and only sub-Saharan African to hold those world records, I've been told by some of them through the years that I am an inspiration. They have encouraged me to write my story so young people in my country of Tanzania, in Africa, and around the world have the opportunity to know me.

I ran my last competitive race more than 30 years ago, and I've put on a few pounds since then. My world records were set almost 50 years ago. What was ground-breaking at the time I did it—just ask the guys I ran against—is rarely discussed now.

I know I'm much more than what happened on two different days out of the more than 69 years and counting that I've been alive. Yet those two days in many ways changed my life forever, and gave me the opportunity to pursue purpose that I hope will outlast me long after I've left the earth.

That's where this book comes in.

You don't have to set world records to create your legacy. That's what I hope you think about as you read my story. No matter what you do in life, no matter what achievements or struggles, if you haven't determined the values you want to uphold, you will have a difficult time discovering your greatest potential and reaching your goals.

That's because if you haven't defined your values, you will waver when something easier comes along to chase. And trust me, you can always find something easier than maintaining the values you've chosen. Values require discipline. The world is not meant to be easy, but you don't have to make it harder by fighting against yourself either.

I was too young when I was racing against the world's best middle-distance runners to fully understand what I'm sharing with you now, but I look back and realize I had already identified the three values that would make me the man I wanted to be—confident, committed, and willing to make sacrifices for a greater good. Those three values sustained me when I won and when I lost, on the track and in other endeavors through the years. They have kept me striving for excellence, especially when difficult times arrive.

My most successful races were just several moments distilled into times on stopwatches out of millions of other moments I've experienced. Each moment gives me a chance to put my values to work in service to myself, my family and friends, and the larger community. Now I have other priorities and goals, and I wake up each day doing my best to achieve them with integrity and humility.

I've clearly identified the three values that sustain those efforts: Confidence. Commitment. Sacrifice. This book is my attempt to share the importance of those with you by sharing the story of my life.

You'll learn about me in these pages. I hope this peek into my experiences will inspire you to apply those values so you can make-moments that create a legacy you and your loved ones will be proud of.

PROLOGUE

Peeking Over My Shoulder

Christchurch, New Zealand, Queen Elizabeth II Park. February 2, 1974.

With barely over a lap to go, I look back—just for a split second—over my right shoulder. About 10 meters back are John Walker and Rod Dixon, both of New Zealand. Ben Jipcho of Kenya is on the inside lane, out of my view, but I know he's lurking.

The American baseball pitcher Satchel Paige famously said, "Don't look back, something might be gaining on you." With all due respect to Satch, he never had the world's best middle-distance runners chasing him down in the 1500m final of the Commonwealth Games.

They are gaining on me, sure. But sometimes a peek back prepares you for what is about to come. People assume a lead runner peeking is getting tired. It's seen as a sign of weakness. I disagree. It actually takes confidence to look around and expose yourself in that way. If you are prepared, that peek is nothing other than a chance to assess the situation.

I look over my shoulder because it will help me plot my next moves. I may or may not be struggling—I certainly try not to show it either way—but I need to know where the competition is. Racing is not unlike business or any other sport. You prepare as best you can and control the variables you can control, but ultimately you'll have to respond to what your competitors do.

The bell sounds as I lead the field of 11 men into the final 400 meters of what is shaping up to be called "the most glorious metric mile in history." I had tried to bury them with a blistering pace right from the gun, and I have indeed pushed them to their limits. But I'm not yet out of their reach.

As Dixon said later, "Once he set his pace and wasn't running away, I knew we had the potential to catch him with 600 meters to go. I felt we would catch him—strength in numbers. He was the hunted and knew it."

It's true. The antelope knows the pack wants him for dinner, but that doesn't mean he's helpless. He must be ready when the lions prepare to pounce.

I accelerate into the curve and put a little more gap between me and my pursuers, knowing I have trained strong and smart enough that I still have another gear if I need it down the stretch. I know I'm ready.

The next 55.4 seconds will transform my life. I'm 20 years old and about to be introduced to the world.

PART ONE

In the Shadow of Kilimanjaro

Filbert Bayi, early 1970s.

CHAPTER 1

My Mother and the Hyenas

I WAS RACING BEFORE I WAS EVEN OUT OF THE WOMB. MY MOTHER—as all mothers do—did the hard work, and I guess you could say we lost that race from Karatu to Mbulu. But as I grew up and learned the details of our journey, I realized just how determined and caring my mother was as I developed in her belly.

My father was a cowherder in Karatu, a village on the road from Mount Kilimanjaro and Arusha to the savannas and millions of animals that live in the Serengeti. He traveled extensively throughout the region to buy and sell his stock. When my mother was seven months pregnant with me, my father's business partner returned from an auction in Mbulu, 77 kilometers (48 miles) away, with a grave message: my father was seriously ill and too weak to return home.

Unsure just how bad his condition was, my mother immediately decided she needed to see him. In 1953 in rural Tanganyika, as my home country of Tanzania was known at the time, she had no transportation options other than to go on foot. So she did.

My father's brother accompanied her as they followed the cow path south, through the bush and past the volcanic craters that dotted the landscape west of Lake Manyara. They left in early morning and walked nearly a marathon's distance for two days in a row. Though they were then near the tiny village of Kansay, where my great uncle and his family lived, they were too tired to reach his property and instead found a spot to sleep outside overnight.

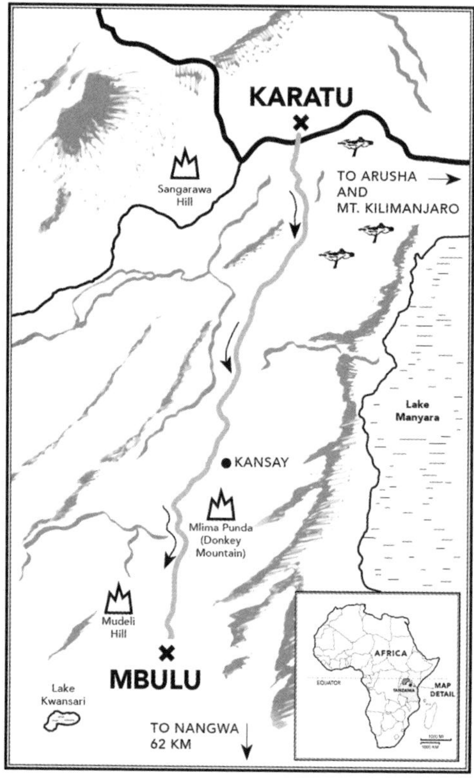

Karatu to Mbulu. Tanganyika, 1953.

When night fell, they could hear hyenas laughing all around them. Staying calm and quiet, they wondered just how close the pack was. At times, they said, it felt like the hyenas were just a few bushes away from them. In the womb, I didn't cause her additional trouble by kicking her or putting her in pain that would draw the hyenas' attention to them. When the sun came up the next day and the hyenas had ended their growling and giggling, my mother and uncle resumed the journey, passing Mlima Punda (Swahili for "Donkey Mountain") along the way and finally arriving in Mbulu around sunset.

//

My mother, Magdalena Qwaray, was a teenager threading leather when she met Bayi Sanka Irafay. He was visiting the goat auction at the market in her village of Nangwa, and making clothes was her small business at that market. Nangwa is 142 kilometers (88 miles) south of Karatu, in Manyara Region, and Bayi was Mwriaqw, a member of the Iraqw ethnic group, while Magdalena was Barabaig.

He was not deterred by either the distance or their ethnic differences. Bayi told her that when he returned to Nangwa, he would take her home with him. Several months later, he was back in Nangwa for another goat auction and sure enough, Bayi was true to his word. He met Magdalena's parents and asked for her hand in marriage, offering a substantial dowry of cows for their young daughter that they accepted.

Magdalena was a village girl but ready to move away from her family to Karatu. Bayi owned goats and cows and was doing well in business. She expected to be healthy and wealthy with him for many years to come and raise a big family together—"to go to good pasture," as the saying goes.

//

When Magdalena reached Mbulu after two long days of walking, her hopes of seeing her husband and helping him regain his health were quickly dashed. He was already dead and buried. She never even saw his body in Mbulu. But she stayed strong, as she always has for me. My father was a healthy man in his late 20s, so the news was a shock. Several people who tended to him at the end told her he was foaming at the mouth and suggested he had been poisoned. This seemed far-fetched. He was successful enough as a cowherder, but what did anyone stand to gain from his death?

My mother and uncle left with no firm answers. They took care of matters in Mbulu and began the two-day journey back to Karatu. When they stayed with my great-uncle near Kansay on the return trip, she had to be isolated, as required by her Barabaig tribal mourning custom. Any plates or cups she used were thrown away after she used them.

When she arrived home, the reality of her new life became clear. She had cows and crops to tend to, with no husband to share the joys and burdens of a baby on the way. Fortunately, her small hut on my grandfather Sanka's land was still a safe place to call home. My uncle and his wife lived close by, and they made sure my mother had support, including helping me come into the world healthy.

As I grew up, my aunt and uncle took care of both of us. When they had children later—eventually eight—I considered these my six brothers and two sisters rather than my younger cousins, and I have always called them so. My father's brother and his family were always very good to us.

My mother, Magdalena Qwaray, in Karatu, 2021.

Still, as I got older, even in a community where families helped one another to survive, I often felt that my mom and I were on our own and had to rely on each other. I think it's why we were so close then and have been my whole life. She still lives in Karatu. Three of my younger brothers and one of her granddaughters take care of her, but trust me… Magdalena Qwaray is as resourceful and resolute as ever. I see her several times a year when I take the 45-minute flight from Dar es Salaam to the Mount Kilimanjaro Airport between Moshi and Arusha.

She doesn't know exactly how old she is—"I think I'm 200 years old," she jokes. She remembers all of this, and she is unimpressed at her age, noting that around Kilimanjaro you can find people who live to be 105 years old or even older. They eat healthy food and live in a moderate climate. Why wouldn't they live that long, she asks?

She downplays that long walk when she carried me across the rugged countryside in her belly, saying she did what had to be done. But even when I first heard the story as a little boy, I recognized it was an act of sacrifice for the sake of her family—the first of thousands of examples of my mother's strength and sacrifices for me.

My mother determined after her heartbreaking trip to Mbulu that I would be named Habiye, which is the Barabaig word for "hyena." I was born on June 22, 1953, in Karatu and soon received my full Christian name of Filbert Bayi Sanka when I was baptized. My proper surname was my grandfather's name, Sanka, but when I was in town or at school, people usually called me by my father's name, Bayi, a traditional name which was easier to remember than the Christian name of Filbert. Over time, even though Sanka remains on my passport, I became most commonly known as Filbert Bayi. My mother continued to call me Habiye…even when nobody else did. Because of her, I still consider it my nickname, and I have always identified with hyenas—*habiyet*—as a reminder of my first long-distance journey.

Hyenas are revered by some as intelligent, adaptable, and relentless, working together in clans to wear down their prey, even much larger animals, over many miles. An East African Tabwa myth suggests the hyena first brought the sun to warm a cold earth. But other folklore says that hyenas are used in witchcraft. In this interpretation, they are cunning yet cowardly, dirty creatures who steal human babies and livestock, and scavenge other predators' kill. Look up famous quotes about hyenas, and you will see it is these negative views of the animal that predominate. Consider the hyena's violent behavior in Yann Martel's best-selling book and award-winning film *Life of Pi*, or the willingness of hyenas to do Scar's bidding in the Disney film *The Lion King*.

Their trademark laughter, used to communicate with each other, is often used by humans to suggest the hyenas are creating fear or mischief.

It may sound strange for me to identify positively with them, but the tribe my father came from believes that their Iraqw ancestors can influence the living, appearing in the form of a hyena when they do so.

When I think of hyenas, I wonder if they sensed my mother's presence and thoughtfully left her alone to do what she needed to do—find her husband, then mourn him and give birth to her first and only child. I realize how aggressive they could have been to hunt my mother and uncle to keep me from ever leaving my mother's stomach. Were they that kind? Or just not hungry that night? Maybe they found more appealing options.

To me, they symbolize my mother's courage. Though I'm sure she was scared, they provided a young woman some company on a night when her whole world hung in the balance.

CHAPTER 2

My Ancestors' Journey to the Cradle of Humankind

I HAVE NEVER SEEN A PHOTO OF MY FATHER. MY MOTHER CAN TELL ME that I looked like him when I was a young man or that I am a hard worker as he was. I'm sure relatives told me long-forgotten stories about him, but I'll never know how close the resemblance is, physically or in personality and tendencies. The reality is I have no personal recollection of a man who died just weeks before I entered the world.

When I was young, I was told that his Iraqw ancestors—*my* ancestors—made their own epic journey: migrating from Mesopotamia in what is modern-day Iraq to the Horn of Africa, following the eastern branch of the Great Rift Valley that cuts through Somalia, Ethiopia, Kenya, and Tanzania, some continuing even farther south to Mozambique. Further archaeological and anthropological research has cast doubt on this theory, but the Iraqw probably did start traveling from Ethiopia more than 2,000 years ago...still a significant journey.

The Iraqw language has been classified as Southern Cushitic, which would link my ancestors with ethnic groups that settled in the Horn of Africa and Egypt. In fact, when I see Somalis and Ethiopians today, I sometimes feel like I'm looking at a version of myself and the people around me when I was growing up. The Iraqw traveled south along the Rift Valley, eventually settling into the Ngorongoro and Karatu areas of what is today north-central Tanzania, between lakes Manyara and Eyasi.

I saw intelligence and fortitude in the Karatu community where I grew up; the Iraqw have proof of their ingenuity in the ruins of Engaruka, about 80 kilometers (50 miles) north of my birthplace.

If my ancestors are known for one achievement, it's Engaruka. Located in the northern part of the Arusha Region, Engaruka is an intricate canal system developed around the 15th century on the valley's steep slopes. My ancestors channeled water from the Mbulu Highlands of the rift using stone blocks for terracing—reaching almost 10 meters (33 feet) high in some places! It was a clever example amid a harsh environment of adapting with nature rather than working against it. Irrigation allowed inhabitants to efficiently redistribute water to their millet and sorghum fields at the foot of the escarpment. The construction and improvements occurred over three centuries, showing sophisticated technology that allowed agriculture to thrive and the people of this mountainous region to dramatically increase their population.

Though Engaruka was abandoned in the mid-18th century, modern Iraqw stone-walled canals, dams, and furrows are very similar to Engaruka. The Maasai—one of the largest of well over 100 ethnic groups that live in Tanzania today—are commonly seen in this part of the Arusha Region now. Distinctive by their colorful robes as they tend to their cows, goats, and sheep, and revered for their strict warrior culture, Maasai are perhaps the most prominent vision of what Kenyan and Tanzanian ethnic groups look like to much of the world. Maasai entered the region from the center of the continent around the time Engaruka stopped being cultivated; their stories attest that the Iraqw were already established in Arusha when the Maasai arrived.

When I was a boy, I never strayed more than 48 kilometers (30 miles) from home, and that was only when herding cows from one grazing land to the next. Today the Iraqw and many other ethnic groups that make up Tanzania are not as homogenous as when I was growing up. Among other factors, the modern world and intermarriage—which my Iraqw father and Barabaig mother are examples of—have made ethnic affiliations fuzzier and less important. We are a unified republic with a national language, Swahili, that brings us together. Still, there are nearly half a million Iraqw, which makes it one of the top two dozen in terms of population among Tanzanian ethnic groups. Their journey many years ago brought me there, just as my mother's did in 1953.

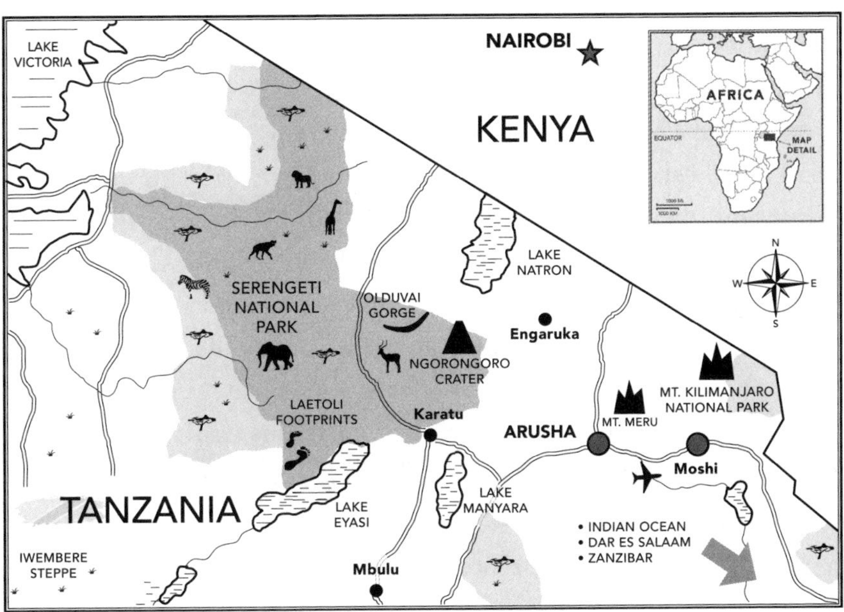

Geologic features of northern Tanzania.

My young life was strictly ordered by the seasons and sheltered from the outside world, but we heard stories of the ancient cultures that had lived in the region before us. Engaruka was only one of many major archaeological sites that surrounded us. Northern Tanzania is known today for the incredible variety of animals that roam the Serengeti plains and Ngorongoro Crater, as well as the majestic Mount Kilimanjaro that towers 5,895 meters (19,341 feet). I grew up in the middle of all of those natural wonders. But the human history of the region is just as dramatic and fascinating as volcanoes, rhinos, and zebras.

It's a storied area that dates back many millennia before the arrival of the Iraqw. Olduvai Gorge stretches along the western edge of the

Ngorongoro Conservation Area for 48 kilometers (30 miles) and has been a treasure chest of fossils and stone tools for archaeologists over the past century. Olduvai traces early human species, including *Homo habilis* (1.9 million years ago) and *Homo erectus* (1.2 million years ago). *Homo habilis* was one of the first hominid species that could make stone tools, a development that helped ensure our chances of long-term survival so we could get to our own species, *Homo sapiens.*

Not that I knew about it, but world-famous archaeologists Mary and Louis Leakey were excavating Olduvai near my home when I was a little boy. They visited in 1953, the year I was born, and again in 1955, 1957, and 1959. Because of discoveries made at Olduvai, scientists took a great leap forward in understanding how our ancestors increased their cognitive capacities to communicate with one another, develop tools, build communities, and begin transitioning to human form and behavior.

Dating back even further before our big brains are the Laetoli Footprints. Located about 48 kilometers (30 miles) from Olduvai, they were found by Mary Leakey and her team in 1978. Those 70 early human footprints were preserved in wet volcanic ash over 27 meters (30 yards)—a distance barely long enough for Usain Bolt to reach full stride, but a vitally important discovery for humankind. At the time, they were the oldest known evidence of humans walking upright on two legs—3.6 million years ago. Unlike apes, which use their massive big toes for locomotion, these early humans showed that they were perhaps the first heel-strikers, a noteworthy development for anyone interested in the beginnings of our species...and perhaps for shoe-company representatives.

Clearly, we all have been running a very long time.

CHAPTER 3

Discovering Independence

I SPENT MUCH OF MY TIME AS A BOY DOING CHORES ON THE SMALL farm in Karatu that my grandfather Sanka had originally settled, herding cows and goats in the bush.

Even before I first started going to primary school at age eight, I was working. We had no machinery to work the several acres of land, so I got to know how to use a hoe very well. My mother never remarried. Tradition dictated that my widowed mother would be cared for by my uncle, which he did. But he was married with his own children, so my first memories are of my mom and me taking care of each other. She was a hard worker and expected the same from me. This was good. It made me strong and encouraged me to help her without question and do what was needed to get the job done.

First and foremost, this meant herding. Some days my cousins Martin and Qwaydimi (whom I called brothers) and a few other boys would leave at 5 a.m. to drive the cows to grass or salt that was anywhere from 10 to 25 kilometers (6.2 to 15.5 miles) away, then drive them back home. If we were lucky, the cows would move fast enough that we could get home before dark. Sometimes we needed to whistle at them or push them or smack their bottoms to keep them going.

Usually, we would have an adult or responsible teenager who was considered to be in charge of us. But it's not like we were getting into trouble. We knew our job was to keep the cows and goats safe. As long as we kept an eye on them and got them where they needed to go, we could do what we wanted.

I was astounded by the noisy giant birds that occasionally flew overhead. Air travel wasn't very common in northern Tanzania in the 1950s and 1960s. I barely comprehended that these tubes were carrying people across the sky—or that I could someday ride in one.

Not surprisingly, we had a lot of time to kill. We'd tell stories, play games, rest in the shade. We also would also play a traditional game where we fought each other with sticks. Each person would hold a stick in each hand, one to try to control or push the opponent where you want him to go and one to hit him. I think it's supposed to make you better at cowherding, but we played it because it was fun.

I've seen similar stick games in Ethiopia and Somalia, played by children who look like they could be my brothers. I believe some of my father's Iraqw ancestors stayed behind in what is now Eritrea, Djibouti, and Kenya. Some of their features, physical and cultural, stayed there as well. Our societies adapted as we responded to our new homes and natural surroundings. The constant human migration is fascinating to me. We know so little about how and why early humans got to where they were going.

My favorite activity in the bush was hunting with my best friend, a mutt named Simba. He wasn't big, but he was sleek and fast. And, man, was he disciplined and loyal. We relied on our dogs if we wanted meat for lunch. The only sticks we had were to tend to the cows, so there were no spears to go after bigger animals like gazelles or even dik-dik. Still, Simba and I loved chasing after them.

Simba chased rabbits through grassy areas until the rabbit found a hole. Even if Simba lost the scent, he always seemed to pick it back up, then keep the rabbit scared and underground until we arrived. We would start digging to flush the rabbit out…right into Simba's waiting teeth.

This type of hunting required Simba and us boys to be consistent and patient. If we had a good day and Simba was careful not to mangle his catch, we made a barbecue and had a hot lunch in the bush.

Old land, new country

My mother and I lived in a mud hut with a grass roof that sat partially underground. It was constructed decades earlier by my family in the traditional Iraqw method. It was intended to fool the Maasai and other enemies who would think it was just a small hill and possibly look past it.

Our home was in the Karatu District off the main road—such as it was back then—going to Ngorongoro Crater and the Serengeti. Now the area is near downtown Karatu, a city of more than 200,000 people. Back then, it was a small farming village. My grandparents were not wealthy, but they did amass enough animals and space to keep them sheltered and would have been considered well off. Property lines weren't clear back then. People stayed put for generations, so if there were boundary disputes, they were dealt with locally. But much of the area was communal anyway, so these arguments were rare.

Grandfather Sanka's land had been split up among his sons. My father's death made maintaining our portion of it more difficult, but we managed. We grew maize and beans and ate mostly vegetables. Though we raised goats and cows, we usually just ate meat when we hunted a gazelle. When I was eight years old, my mother insisted I go to school because she felt an education was the best way for me to help support our family. I complied, but it didn't mean I got to do any less farm work or herding!

My first language is Kiiraqw, but I learned Swahili at the Catholic elementary school. When I grew a little older, we had an English class too, but I don't remember much more than "Good morning" and "What's your name?" I didn't really start to learn English until I was traveling in the 1970s.

Soon after I started school, the Republic of Tanganyika was born. That may seem like a big deal, but it meant nothing to me. The farmers in the area were uneducated. The animals and fields needed tending every day. We knew that British officials were in charge of the Arusha regional government and Karatu District, but we saw no immediate changes to our daily lives after December 9, 1961, when Tanganyika gained sovereignty from the United Kingdom.

Looking back, I realized that this was a very big deal. The whole continent was in the midst of change, either violently or peacefully. After centuries, European colonization was collapsing in Africa. But all I remember about the occasion in Tanganyika was that there was a "marathon" in Karatu celebrating our newfound independence. When I say marathon, I just mean a long race. There was a designated course. It could have been 20 kilometers (12.4 miles) or it could have been 50 kilometers (31 miles). Whatever distance it was, we called it a marathon. It wasn't marked well and it wasn't timed. There was just a winner and the celebration of a new country.

Tanganyika gained the islands of Zanzibar and Pemba just a few years later. Zanzibar had been ruled by Arabs for two centuries but also was a protectorate of the United Kingdom. While Tanganyika gained independence without violence, Zanzibar's joining our country included bloodshed. In December 1963, after the UK ended its protectorate status, it looked like Zanzibar would be an independent country. But a month later, the Sultan was forced into exile by African revolutionaries. Thousands of Arabs and Indians were killed. The Sultanate was replaced by a socialist government led by Abeid Karume.

Tanganyika president Julius Nyerere, a schoolteacher-turned-politician who was one of the few university-educated people in the country at the time, feared that Zanzibar would become a hotspot in the battle between the United States and Soviet Union. Tanganyika tried to maintain a balance between the two Cold War powers, and Nyerere had no desire to bring that conflict to a newly independent and volatile country 80 kilometers (50 miles) off his eastern coast.

On April 26, 1964, the People's Republic of Zanzibar and Pemba, as it was officially known, merged with the mainland to become the United Republic of Tanganyika and Zanzibar. Blending the two names, within a year my country was renamed the United Republic of Tanzania, with Zanzibar retaining autonomous status within it. The Germans and Britons that had ruled the mainland for more than a century and the Arabs that had ruled the island for even longer were no longer in charge.

This was a turbulent time in an otherwise peaceful transition in my country. The Zanzibar-born writer Abdulrazak Gurnah was a teenager when he fled the violence and settled in England. When he won the 2021 Nobel Prize in Literature, the committee that awarded it to him praised his "uncompromising and compassionate penetration of the effects of colonialism and the fate of the refugee in the gulf between cultures and continents."

In his acceptance speech in Stockholm, Sweden, he referenced his childhood experiences under colonial rule, the violence of the Zanzibar Revolution, and life as a refugee:

> I reflected on what I had left behind in the reckless flight from my home. A profound chaos descended on our lives in the mid-1960s, whose rights and wrongs were obscured by the brutalities that accompanied the changes brought about by the revolution in 1964: detentions, executions, expulsions, and endless small and large indignities and oppressions. In the midst of these events and with the mind of an adolescent, it was impossible to think clearly about the historical and future implications of what was happening...
>
> There was also another understanding of history necessary to address, one that became clearer to me when I lived closer to its source in England, clearer than it had been while I was going through my colonised education in Zanzibar. We were, those of our generation, children of colonialism in a way that our parents were not and nor were those who came after us, or at least not in the same way. By that I don't mean that we were alienated from the things our parents valued or that those who came after us were liberated from colonial influence. I mean that we grew up and were educated in that period of high imperial confidence, at least in our parts of the world, when domination disguised its real self in euphemisms and we agreed to the subterfuge. I refer to the period before decolonisation campaigns across the region hit their stride and drew our attention to the depredations of colonial rule. Those who came after us had their post-colonial disappointments and their own self-delusions to comfort them, and perhaps did not see clearly,

> or in great enough depth, the way in which the colonial encounter had transformed our lives, that our corruptions and misrule were in some measure also part of that colonial legacy...
>
> But writing cannot be just about battling and polemics, however invigorating and comforting that can be. Writing is not about one thing, not about this issue or that, or this concern or another, and since its concern is human life in one way or another, sooner or later cruelty and love and weakness become its subject. I believe that writing also has to show what can be otherwise, what it is that the hard domineering eye cannot see, what makes people, apparently small in stature, feel assured in themselves regardless of the disdain of others. So I found it necessary to write about that as well, and to do so truthfully, so that both the ugliness and the virtue come through, and the human being appears out of the simplification and stereotype. When that works, a kind of beauty comes out of it.

Gurnah and I have lived vastly different experiences, though we both were born in the country now known as Tanzania. I think it's important to acknowledge the Zanzibar Revolution and not diminish it. Gurnah was an Arab-born Muslim on a colonized island that was later subsumed by a mainland government, which forced him into exile. I was born of rural parents from different ethnic groups and raised Christian in a colonized country whose newly independent mainland government subsumed his. I'm five years younger than him, which during a time of massive upheaval is a lifetime in terms of recognition and perception of the world.

If I met him, I don't know that we would agree on a lot. We may not have much to discuss at all. However, I do know that we both showed a commitment to excellence in our chosen fields, made sacrifices in the process of doing so, and developed the confidence to reach our goals that led to achieving international praise. I deeply respect his commitment to writing so that people are not forgotten and have pride in themselves, that out of "the ugliness and the virtue...the human being appears out of the simplification and stereotype." That is how we learn about each other and choose compassion and understanding. Gurnah is correct: beauty does come out of that.

Perhaps we would have plenty to talk about after all.

Nyerere's tactical goal of unifying Tanganyika and Zanzibar was to moderate the external socialist influence in our new country from the Soviets and Chinese. But he was not willing to be a pawn for the United States and western powers either. Tanzania's efforts to find its footing amid Cold War politics became apparent to me later, in the politicized sporting world of the 1970s and 1980s.

Instead of Soviet-style socialism or American capitalism, Nyerere instituted African-centered socialist policies on health, education, and social welfare. Nyerere used the concept of *ujamaa*, which translates to "extended family" or "familyhood," to emphasize the importance of community and cooperative economics in governance.

Ujamaa in action was best expressed in the Tanzania African National Union's 1967 Policy on Socialism and Self Reliance document, which became known as the Arusha Declaration. It was developed by Nyerere and the political party he helped form way back in 1954 and quickly became a point of pride for my young country. It included a one-party system under TANU; compulsory education; institutionalization of social, economic, and political equality; abolition of discrimination; and nationalization of the economy and villagization of production.

When Nyerere was asked by *New Internationalist magazine* in 1999 just months before he died if the Arusha Declaration was still relevant, he replied, "I still travel around with it. I read it over and over to see what I would change. Maybe I would improve on the Kiswahili that was used but the Declaration is still valid: I would not change a thing...The Arusha Declaration was what made Tanzania distinctly Tanzania."

There are some who might think Tanganyika, and then Tanzania, was on the wrong path with socialism. As an adult, I studied history and saw it as a necessary step in the transition. I have been an advocate of hard work and competition, which are hallmarks of capitalism, but I believe the communal aspects of socialism better represent the mindset of Africa's many cultures and societies. I understand why a continent in the midst of a postcolonial revolution in the 1960s would be drawn to governmental structures that were centralized.

Above all, despite the Zanzibar Rebellion, I'm happy to say that Tanzania's path to the future was more peaceful than that of many African countries. I've negotiated and partnered with governments of all sizes and ideologies for many years, as a school administrator, as an influential local leader, and in the Olympic movement. I don't have strong political views about what constitutes a more just society. I believe you must have ethical and well-intentioned people in power, regardless of the governmental structure, and they must be held accountable to the public through regular and fair elections. A government is no better or worse than the people who occupy political office, and those people represent—for better or worse—the constituents who vote for them.

My family didn't lose our land during this transition period, but others did. The government encouraged people to move to Karatu, and they were enticed to do so with farmland gifted by Nyerere's policies. It wasn't hard for the government to seize and redistribute land, since there were rarely written records of official ownership. Before long, Karatu grew to be a substantial city.

I was a 10-year-old boy living in the highlands, far from the political maneuverings happening along the coast in the capital of Dar es Salaam. My only memory of the union of the two countries is hearing about the symbolic gesture of mainland soil and island sand being mixed by the leaders on Zanzibar to signal a unified Tanzania. That felt hopeful. Whether you're a cowherding boy or a new nation, independence is a wonderful opportunity. But it is not just a single celebratory moment. Independence must be cultivated over and over again.

Milk money

Independence comes with responsibility. I spent a lot of time on my own, and usually I was quite good at taking care of my chores. My mother rarely needed to discipline me, but when I made a mistake, she was quick to punish me.

We used to sell our milk to people in the village, and I would make those deliveries. Glass bottles were difficult to come by and an essential part of our business, so they were a valuable commodity. An important task when making deliveries was to bring back the empties to be washed out and re-used.

One time on my way back home from deliveries, I came across some boys playing marbles. I wanted to join them, but I first decided to hide the bottles in the grass a little way from the circle. I didn't want to have to keep my eye on the bottles while I was shooting marbles, and I knew glass was a target for theft.

This seemed responsible to me. But when I finished playing, I completely forgot about the bottles. When I reached home, my mother asked me where they were. I told her I had lost them. She beat me to hell! She was furious and had every right to be. I knew that having to replace bottles was an unnecessary expense, and perhaps could result in wasted milk if we couldn't get it bottled in time because we lacked containers. The next day, I returned to the spot where I had been playing. I found my hiding place, and fortunately they were still there. I brought the bottles to her. We were able to laugh about it, but she made it clear that I had better have learned my lesson.

I did.

On foot everywhere

I spent much of my childhood using my feet to carry me—no bikes, no buses, certainly no cars—all at mile-high elevation. When we took the cows and goats to graze, I might go 10–25 kilometers (6–15 miles) one way, not to mention the running to keep cows contained, go hunting, or goof around. The Catholic school was just over three kilometers (two miles) away, and I would come home for lunch and then return in the afternoon for a total of nearly 13 kilometers (eight miles).

Most people in Karatu were Lutheran or Catholic. My mom was devout and made sure we went every Sunday, which I enjoyed. That was also a six-kilometer round trip (four miles).

No question this built stamina in my body, but I don't overstate the importance of this upbringing when I answer people about why I was successful as a runner. Everybody ran and walked those kinds of distances to get from place to place in bare feet or flimsy sandals made of animal skin or car tires. What choice did we have?

People look for simple answers to explain cause and effect. I enjoyed the freedom of being on my own and responsible for my own transportation, so running didn't feel like a burden to me. Maybe it did to others. I created games for myself and with others to pass the time. Being on foot meant an opportunity to have fun and, I soon discovered, to travel. If there was a benefit that I gained from my upbringing, it was that: running equaled freedom and fun, which made me want to do more of it. That just made me better at it and more motivated to keep doing it as I got older.

I played all the activities available to me as a kid. Everyone wanted to be a football star, but we also enjoyed tug-of-war games and a traditional mancala board game called *bao*. I was a good runner and jumper in athletics meets and also a decent football player. Often, we would use a ball made of old clothing we wound together. I wasn't too bad at basketball either, even though I was one of the shorter guys. I certainly didn't think I was destined to be a great runner. My first distance races were in 1964, and I competed in my first regional championships in Arusha a few months later. This was a thrill. I considered it a privilege to get to represent Karatu in athletics, and it became an annual excursion.

We took a bus and rode 140 kilometers (87 miles) east to the biggest city in the area. One opponent in those regional meets was Alexander Stephen Akwhari, whose older brother John Stephen Akwhari was Tanzania's top marathoner at the time. Alexander was from Mbulu, the village where my father died, and was a good athlete in his own right. I was always near the front in the mile and the 880-yard dash, but he made sure I didn't win them.

A grandmother's love

My life took a scary turn in 1966. I was coughing a lot and my family couldn't lower my fever. I tried to remain active, but I started spitting blood and soon they determined that I had contracted tuberculosis. Suddenly, running and school and farm work had to be put on hold.

I don't know for certain how I was attacked by TB, but we had livestock under the same roof as us and I spent a lot of time taking care of goats and cows. I assume I inhaled their air in the enclosed space and it got into my lungs. I was taken to the closest major hospital, in Mbulu, by a tractor pulling me in a trailer. This was the same 77-kilometer journey my mother had walked when I was in her belly 13 years earlier, but this time it was a dirt road that vehicles could use, not just a narrow path.

My grandmother accompanied me on the trip and then stayed in Mbulu with relatives for the month I was there. She walked eight kilometers (five miles) each way, arriving first thing in the morning each day when visitors were allowed at the hospital. She brought me porridge and milk, and just as importantly, my grandmother gave me a familiar and loving face I could talk to instead of staring at those sterile walls all day long. After a month I was able to return home, but I wasn't allowed to go back to school and risk infecting my classmates, so I had to repeat that grade.

I've been asked if contracting tuberculosis made me more susceptible to malaria, which I had severe reactions to over the years while I was racing competitively. I was told that I should expect a full recovery from TB, and I trained well once I was healthy again, so I always embraced the mindset that TB was in the past. I didn't want to introduce negative thoughts; remembering those hard times was counterproductive for me. I wanted to erase that period of time from my memory.

Now that I'm older though, I must admit that TB attacks the whole cardiopulmonary system. It's not unreasonable to think that malaria was ready to pounce more readily in me than others. I never spent much of my brain power worrying about it, however. Then and now, I can't control how my body's immune system responds beyond doing my best to stay healthy.

I learned a couple lessons from that teenage experience. First, a grandmother's love is powerful. I guess I found out where my mother got her big heart, intensity, and self-discipline. Second, my mom and I were not truly alone. Besides my grandmother staying with me, my mom received support from the community in helping with chores when I was away. Our friends at the Catholic church provided prayers and food.

I strongly believe in the individual virtues of sacrifice, commitment, and confidence when it comes to reaching your goals. Any of us must choose these to find success. But we are better able to accomplish these values when we have the support of our closest friends and family. Seek out ways to support others, and you will find you have more support than you ever realized.

Creating my own life

The changes that have occurred in my and my mother's lifetime are astonishing to me. The Barabaig and Iraqw people used to have a tenuous peace to help ward off the Maasai when those warriors entered their homelands in the 19th century. But my mom (a Barabaig) married my dad (an Iraqw), and all three of those groups have intermarried and intermingled and coexisted for decades now with very little concern about any of our ethnicities. Even on small farms, the technological advances mean work can now get done in a fraction of the time it took me to do tasks by hand as a small boy. The vaccines and medical possibilities to deal with tuberculosis or malaria—or for that matter, a worldwide pandemic like COVID-19—mean many people can be saved before more damage is done.

It used to take a couple days on foot or by tractor to get to the nearest hospital. Now I fly from my home outside Dar es Salaam to visit my mom in Karatu in less than an hour. And speaking of airplanes, I soon would learn the inner workings of those noisy giant birds and I've flown to cities all over the world more times than I can count. I learned not just from my parents and their ancestors but from my own experiences growing up in the shadow of Kilimanjaro how to create a life that was my own.

First though, I had to make a difficult decision—leaving home.

CHAPTER 4

Serving My Country

ONE OF THE FIRST TANZANIANS IN THE OLYMPICS FINISHED LAST—and his effort was as memorable as almost any other in the history of the modern Games.

The story of John Stephen Akhwari has been told many times, thanks to Bud Greenspan's documentary *100 Years of Olympic Glory*. Four Tanganyika runners had competed in 1964. Three other Tanzanian runners joined Akhwari for Mexico City 1968, which was the first Olympics in which the United Republic of Tanzania, under its newly recognized national Olympic committee, fielded a team.

I was 15 years old and Tanzania just eight. Even if I hadn't run against his younger brother Alexander in the regional championships, Akhwari's experience was inspiring to my young self and country.

Akhwari was one of the best marathoners in the world at the time, but he struggled that day. He experienced cramps in the high altitude, and then, nearing the midway point of the 26.2-mile race, he was knocked to the ground while runners jostled for position. He dislocated his knee and jammed his shoulder hard into the pavement—but he didn't quit the race. Akhwari continued on to the finish line inside Estadio Olímpico Universitario.

More than an hour after Ethiopian Mamo Wolde won the race with a time of 2 hours, 20 minutes, and 26 seconds, Akhwari was still on the course. The sun had set, Wolde had received his gold medal, and only a few thousand people remained in the stadium. A camera crew got word that one runner remained, and so his slow path toward the finish in the darkness—right leg bandaged haphazardly, and walking steps interspersed with his short limping stride until he ran the entire final lap to the cheers of the crowd that had stayed—was captured for the world to see.

That turned out to be a gift. Greenspan, the award-winning documentarian of the Olympics who was just getting started then, featured Akhwari's finish—57th and last of the 75 who started the race—in his movie. With the majestic "Israel in Egypt" oratorio by Handel playing as Akhwari enters the stadium, generations have now seen Akhwari.

"Afterwards," says the narrator in a godlike voice, "it was written: today we have seen a young African runner who symbolizes the finest in the human spirit, a performance that gives true dignity to sport, a performance that lifts sports out of the category of grown men playing at games, a performance that gives meaning to the word 'courage.' All honor to John Stephen Akhwari of Tanzania."

I've met Akhwari many times through the years. He remained a world-class runner for another decade after Mexico City, memorably placing fifth in the 1970 Commonwealth Games marathon with a time of 2:15:05. More importantly, he made the most of the opportunity that fate gave him. He has lived a simple and meaningful life as a hardworking farmer with a wife and six children. And the world has not forgotten him. John received a National Hero Medal of Honor in 1983 and lent his name to the John Stephen Akhwari Athletic Foundation, which supports Tanzanian athletes training for the Olympics.

He was invited to the 2000 Olympics in Sydney and served as a goodwill ambassador and torchbearer in the torch relay through Dar es Salaam prior to the 2008 Olympics in Beijing.

Leaving home

We all serve our country in different ways. My first chance to do so came soon after John's epic run. As an only child and the oldest of my cousins,

I had always been a good and willing helper at home and on the farm and bush, so my mother was not pleased at the possibility of her only son leaving for the city. My grades in school were good, and she encouraged me to do well there. But she had never received formal education herself and didn't think I needed advanced education beyond the basics. She was tough and a survivor. In her mind, that was enough for me too.

So when I received an opportunity to join the army, it all happened very quickly and caught her off guard. It was May 1970, and the air transport batallion was looking for athletic and academically adept young men to learn about aircraft mechanics and airplane engineering. I didn't consider myself ambitious back then, though I was certainly competitive on the sports fields and proud of my skills in subjects such as physics and chemistry.

The army was offering a new program that would allow me to get my diploma in aircraft mechanics on a condensed schedule. It started before I had finished my studies back home, but I didn't care. This was a chance to do something different with my life.

It left my mother in tears for me to leave home, but I took a bus from Karatu to Dar, 500 miles away, to discover what lay in store. She was proud of me, but she knew she would miss me and wondered if I would ever come back home. In her mind, even though there was no imminent threat of war waiting for me, she thought if I was in the army I would get sent to a danger zone. It was emotionally difficult to leave the most important person in my life behind, but I knew in my heart it was the best thing for me.

Athletics in the army

I wasn't nervous because I was 17 and had no knowledge of how difficult army life would be. I had no grand expectations, so I arrived in Dar open-minded and eager to do my job.

My hard work paid off. We were held to a rigorous schedule with lots of exams to weed out the candidates who weren't able to contribute. There were about 75 of us at the start, and not even 20 remaining by the end of the program. It was a two-year crash course that normally required four years. We took lots of science and engineering courses and learned about electrical systems, engine maintenance, and all aspects of ensuring airplanes were in working order before taking off. My specialty was air frames—checking wings, propellers, fuel, basically anything on the outside of the plane. The focus required for me to handle the details of airplane maintenance translated well to my preparation for running.

I didn't consider myself a runner at the time, despite my modest success back home. In one of my first races as a member of the army squad, I took second place in the 800m in 1970 at an Armed Forces meet in Zanzibar with a time of 1:55.0.

Still, I was really more committed to football (soccer) when I first joined the service. I played the forward position some, and if someone put the ball in front of me I could get a shot on goal because no one could catch me. But creating my own distance was more difficult.

My better position was actually goalkeeper, and I was one of the best in the army. But my interest in football lessened because I didn't want any more abuse! The officials didn't protect goalies very well back then. My small frame got knocked around the box pretty good. I would stick

Me (beside the ball) with the Mbulu Guwang football team in 1970, shortly before joining the army. Mt. Guwang is in the background.

my knee up in the air a lot to protect myself when going up for free balls. Once, in 1971, the air transport wing team was playing one of Tanzania's best clubs. I was on the receiving end of a powerful penalty kick. I stopped the ball in my stomach, but the result was that my gut was in pain for hours afterward. That's when I decided to retire from football. I had no regrets.

Fortunately by then, I was starting to come into my own as a runner. I was selected for the East and Central Africa Athletics Championships just a few months into my army career and boarded one of those giant birds for the first time. The thrill of that first flight with about 10 teammates bound for Lusaka, Zambia, was soon dampened by my subpar performance in the 3000m steeplechase. I didn't finish the race in the dry heat, and it began my decade-long ambivalent relationship with that mysterious event.

Football is a sport that relies on 10 people on the field at any given time. Depending on how you look at it, that's either a blessing or a frustration. I soon realized I liked the self-reliance required by a track and field event. In athletics, you were on your own. I had nobody to blame for my did-not-finish (DNF) except myself, and I resolved to improve my training so it wouldn't happen again.

I managed a promising 3:52 in the 1500m that year. At a regional meet in 1971, we traveled to Zanzibar on a diesel-powered ship. It was slow and the fuel smell just hung in the air. I was sure I would throw up before we docked in Zanzibar Harbor. We arrived and were transported to Beit El-Ras, a never-finished coastal palace for the Sultan of Zanzibar in the 19th century. That sounds luxurious, but it was the army barracks and it served as our training camp and lodging that week. Fortunately, my breakfast had managed to stay down.

As we ran the 1500m, there was a total blackout in Zanzibar Town. My friend Sang Wong, a Chinese-Tanzanian who was a national record holder in the pole vault in the days of aluminum poles, said it was so dark he couldn't even see anybody cross the finish line from where he stood.

Later in our stay, Sang and I slipped out of training camp without permission. Our mission was innocent. We were picking up photos from a studio in Zanzibar Town and he introduced me to his family that lived on the island. When we returned at sunset, armed guards met us at Beit El-Ras. We were detained and given a stern warning before being released...unharmed, a little scared, and much wiser.

Zanzibar is a beautiful place, with its ocean views, coconut and clove plantations, and remnants of a royal past when wealthy sultans ruled. During that era under Abeid Karume, the revolutionary who briefly served as president of Zanzibar before agreeing to be vice President of Tanzania, the island could be ominous as well. But when you are living in military quarters, you follow their regulations and let people know where you are, no matter how stunning the scenery.

My own coach

The army saw me as a potential national-class runner, and I was blessed to be given plenty of time to train and a more well-rounded diet than what I ate in Karatu. In the air wing, I lived in *Nyumbasita* (Swahili for "six houses"). There, I had more autonomy than most privates, who back then were mostly living in tents at the base. It was a privilege, since I was training twice a day in addition to my regular duties. With a refrigerator, I could have eggs, chicken, and other foods available when I wanted to cook rather than having to wait for the dining hall schedule.

What I really enjoyed about running in the army was getting to wear spikes for the first time. After mostly running and jumping with bare feet in athletics meets back home, those six-millimeter pieces of metal digging into the fleshy part of your feet felt like you were the king of the athletes. Even though only thin slabs of sole separated those nubs and your feet, those adidas spikes allowed you to grip the dirt and cinder tracks. When I ran in my first spikes, I was just grateful to have them. I didn't feel the pain until the end of the race.

Despite my much-appreciated spikes and food, what the army didn't offer was a dedicated coach. There were no coaches in Tanzania who had the background or experience to properly train me. The military might consult local club coaches, but they weren't experts. On my first international trip to Zambia, for example, our coach was a Romanian who was employed by the Zanzibar government. I don't recall his name or doing any training with him.

All over the world at that time—in Europe, the United States, the Soviet Union, and New Zealand—knowledge about the physiology and training methods for running was growing by leaps and bounds. Legendary coaches such as Arthur Lydiard, Jack Daniels, Bill Easton, Bill Bowerman, Joe Vigil, and more were experimenting with long, slow distance running and intense interval workouts. They didn't always know what they were doing, but they were figuring it out and passing on that knowledge to their eager running pupils.

Unaware of the newly developing science of running, I became my own coach and took pride in finding ways to improve my performance. I would leave the army base and run through the crowded streets of Dar chasing buses. It became a fun fartlek workout, dodging people and becoming familiar with the routes as I tried to arrive at the next stop before the bus did. I also jogged to the National Stadium to work out there. Back then, there was no security to keep me out, and I could regularly sweat it out on soft cinders.

I was not putting in high mileage. To be honest, I've never enjoyed the long run days. I don't know how many miles I was running each week—a common question for elite distance runners, but I just didn't keep track. I suspect it was not a huge amount by the standards of other runners at the time, but I can say that nearly every one of those miles was quality.

I loved the challenge of going full throttle as long as I could, and I'm certain that paid dividends later on in terms of increasing my aerobic threshold. At the time, it just seemed intuitive to push myself hard whenever I put on my shoes, and then to relax as much as I could when my body was tired and when I was off duty at the base. As an aircraft mechanic—Private First Class—I kept busy ensuring our planes were in good working condition, but I never partied much when I had time off.

For example, I've rarely consumed alcohol in my life. Back home in Karatu, neighbors would help each other with chores and harvest.

I was successful in one of my first attempts at the 3000m steeplechase. Here, I lapped some other participants at the 1971 Tanzania Army Games in Zanzibar.

As a thank-you, a local brew made of millet and maize was a common gift. It was never a big deal whether people drank or chose not to; I never felt peer pressure. My cousins drank when they were old enough. My mother drank. Many of my fellow soldiers drank. Drinking alcohol just never appealed to me. I saw how badly people behaved when they were drunk, and I did not want to be like that.

Finding my form of service

As I saw myself improving on the track and as I gained and gave respect to my fellow airmen, my belief in myself grew. My experience in the army was very positive. I was disciplined, capable, and determined when I was part of something I believed in. It felt like a natural extension of my childhood to be counted on to perform my job and take pride in it. My service formed for me a life philosophy in which I believed commitment, sacrifice, and confidence worked together as essential factors to achieve what I wanted to in life. They shaped me into who I became and how I see myself to this day.

My running was another natural extension of my work ethic. Running was the venue where these three factors came together. In training or in racing, I embodied these traits to the best of my ability. Yes, being an aircraft mechanic in the army was one form of serving my country, and I took it seriously. But I believed my developing talent as an athlete was an equally important form of service. As my superiors occasionally reminded me, it could be an even more impactful opportunity as an example of Tanzanian success in the public eye.

It was the 1970s, so amateurism was still the rule of the day in Olympic sports; I couldn't see track as a professional career. I did, however, see the Olympics as a realistic possibility and a goal that I was now driven to reach. I was one of the fastest middle-distance runners in Tanzania, and I had a shot to be at the 1972 Munich Games—Tanzania's second appearance in the modern Olympics—just as John Stephen Akwhari had paved the way in 1968.

We humans think the ultimate goal is to be the first—to be remembered for being better than everybody else. Sometimes, as Akwhari had shown the world, the braver act is to just keep going. Our destinies can take many shapes.

It actually took me a long time before I heard about Akhwari's race. There were no televisions in Karatu, nor live radio coverage of the marathon. Even if there had been, the broadcast would not have continued once the winner crossed the finish line. We didn't see newspapers every day either. It took word of mouth before I heard about his unwavering commitment. Akhwari will forever be remembered when people talk about the Olympics, not just because of his strong effort but for his response after the event.

"Perhaps the words of John Stephen Akhwari epitomize all that is right in the human spirit," says the narrator in *100 Years of Olympic Glory* as Akhwari reaches the finish line. "When asked why he did not quit, he said simply, 'My country did not send me 5,000 miles to start the race. They sent me 5,000 miles to finish the race.'"

His example made me proud of my country. I can't say that his performance made me immediately start running with competitive purpose or go to sleep each night with Olympic dreams. That took a few more years. Over time, though, I came to believe his example played a role as I set bigger and bigger goals.

And as I developed a strict training regimen in the army and got serious about running, my goals were becoming as big as the moon.

PART TWO

Setting the Pace

Halfway through the 1500m world record in Christchurch, 1974.

CHAPTER 5

The New Kid in Munich

In English, there is a saying: "Necessity is the mother of invention." I didn't know that when I was young and I don't know of an equivalent in Swahili now, but I took those words to heart with my experience at the Olympic Games in 1972. I turned disappointment into a race strategy that would secure my athletics legacy in the years to come.

At that time, the young Tanzanian Olympic committee chose its delegation for the trip to Munich through a national time trial held just a week before the Olympics were to begin. This didn't seem like the best way to prepare athletes for a solid performance on the biggest stage in the world, but it was how it was done. Even more daunting, I had barely ever competed in these events before, and they would be run within an hour of one another in the humidity of our seaside capital city, Dar es Salaam.

I had competed in mile races before, but in the Olympics it is the "metric mile"—the 1500m run—which is 100 meters shorter. I also was selected for the 3000m steeplechase. With times at the national meet of 3:45.6 in the 1500 and 8:55 in the steeplechase, I was considered Tanzania's best chance to reach the final in both events, but I was completely inexperienced. Outside my country, I was unknown.

Truly, I had no idea what to expect. I had just turned 19 years old, and though I had five sprinters, a marathoner, and eight boxer teammates with me as I boarded the plane for my second flight and first-ever trip out of Africa in August 1972, I was figuring everything out as I went by intuition and observation.

I continued doing workouts on dirt and sand roads through the streets of Dar and on the cinder track at the National Stadium. Even if I was there with other army runners, I was almost always training alone. I didn't know the importance of interval training—I raced buses and put in short bursts of speed to entertain myself, then rested while passengers boarded and departed the bus. My pre-Olympic regimen was pretty much just logging mileage, about 16 to 20 kilometers (10 to 12 miles) most days. Shortly before Munich, I met Werner Kramer on the track. Kramer was an East German who was in the country to coach the University of Dar es Salaam track team. But our meeting was too late in the training cycle to benefit me.

Officially, the Tanzanian athletics coach for the Olympic team was Elias Mfungo Sulus. He distinguished himself as a teacher and later became the president of the Tanzania Amateur Athletics Association (TAAA). However, he was not experienced in distance running and didn't have much advice to offer me as I prepared for the biggest competition of my sporting life.

In particular, the steeplechase concerned me. This odd event required the ability to smoothly go over 28 hurdles plus seven water jumps for nearly two miles, ideally without breaking stride so that your momentum keeps carrying you down the track.

It takes years to master this, not weeks. I was not an ideal fit for the steeplechase. My hurdling technique was not efficient, and I was smaller than most of the top runners in the event. Still, my agility from my time on the football pitch and my footspeed were strengths.

Once in Munich, I got a quick education. International races with two dozen of the fastest men in the world jumping over barriers and into water pits meant I was jostling for position constantly. These were experienced racers who had trained four years for their big moment, and

Showing my hurdling form early in my career, here I am (858) in the first heat of the 3000m steeplechase on September 1, 1972, at the Munich Olympiastadion. I placed ninth and didn't advance.

they weren't giving an inch. I spent a lot of energy trying find space for myself that should have been spent propelling my body forward. Even though I bettered my time from the national championships by 14 seconds with a time of 8:41.4—a time I was told later was unofficially the best ever recorded by a 19-year-old up to that date—I was eliminated with a ninth-place showing in the preliminary heat.

I was unable to aggressively attack the hurdles with so many men around me, which meant between the jumps I was adjusting to the conditions instead of accelerating. I was hemmed in with energy ready to burn and nowhere to expend it. That made me angry, which has never been an emotion I feel very often or strongly, or for very long. Life moves on, whether you're ready for it or not. You only interrupt that forward flow when you try to fight it, and the world does not slow down for anybody. I move through the anger by analyzing the results and asking myself what I could have done differently, and within a couple of days I had done just that. I was excited to have a second chance—and in an event that didn't require hurdling.

Unfortunately, any residual anger or anxiety was quickly replaced by sadness. The steeplechase prelim was held on September 1 and my 1500m heat was scheduled for one week later, on September 8.

In between, in the early-morning hours of September 5, one of the most tragic episodes in Olympic history captured the world's attention. While the Olympic Village slept, eight members of the Palestinian terrorist group Black September snuck into the Israeli Olympic delegation's compound, killing two people and taking nine more hostage. The terrorists demanded the release of Palestinian prisoners, and after a dramatic standoff at the airport, all nine Israeli hostages, five of the captors, and one West German police officer were dead.

The whole incident was over in less than 24 hours, but the ramifications in Israel, West Germany, the Arab world, and the Olympic movement would linger for decades.

The Tanzanian dorms were just one apartment over from the Israelis. I was on the pathway between the two buildings in the complex, headed over to the track for an early-morning training session. It was simple to walk anywhere you wanted to go. I noticed people on the second-floor balcony with stockings or masks that seemed to be covering their whole heads. An official told me I needed to return to my block and I noticed a helicopter overhead, but it was all calm. I was annoyed that I couldn't go for a run, but I was clueless about the tragedy developing just a hundred yards away.

The West German government prepared for its big moment on the world stage in 1972 fully aware of the global disdain for how Adolf Hitler used the 1936 Berlin Olympics as propaganda. That and World War II were in the not-too-distant past. Given another chance, the Germans wanted to show openness and hospitality to their guests—they even nicknamed the event "the cheerful Olympics." Security was very light.

A few hours later, more helicopters were circling and people were talking about terrorists in the Olympic Village. It's not as though they were hiding. The terrorists were easy to see right outside the window. Still, few details were known and sporting events continued through much of the day. It took a while for the gravity of the situation to set in, but by early afternoon, the television coverage focused solely on the hostage crisis and continued until the botched late-night rescue attempt at the airport.

I remember my surprise the next day when International Olympic Committee President Avery Brundage announced that after a 24-hour tribute, the games would go on.

It was an impossible situation for everyone. When the qualifying heat came around in the 1500m, I resolved to compartmentalize my emotions. I prayed for the victims and their families, but there was nothing more I could do for them at that moment. I came to Munich to do my best, and this was my second Olympic opportunity to do so. Unfortunately, I got knocked around again. These were high stakes. Everyone desperately wanted to make it into the finals, and I was not prepared for the elbowing and shoving. I got boxed in early, and with that many competitors in less than four laps, it's difficult to escape when you're stuck.

Leading John Kirkbride of Great Britain at the Munich Olympiastadion on September 8, 1972. I placed sixth in the prelims and didn't advance, ending my first Olympics.

I even was initiated into the international middle-distance running community by getting spiked, not an uncommon event for these veteran racers but something I had never even really considered. I placed sixth in my prelims race, bettering my time at the national meet at 3:45.4 but not making the qualifying time to advance to the finals.

//

My first Olympic experience was over too quickly, and I was disappointed with my performance. Considering my lack of experience, I really couldn't be too upset with my showing, though. I improved from my first races in Dar in the 1500m and steeplechase to my second races in Munich, and I knew my inability to reach the finals was not from being unable to keep up; it was about understanding tactics. I *could* do something about that. I was young and determined to make a change, and I expected to have many more opportunities to make the finals and maybe even medal at the Olympics.

I got labeled the "Tiny Tanzanian," which was true. Even among rail-thin distance runners, I was light and little—just under six feet tall and weighing 59 kg (130 pounds). When I returned home, I vowed to run from the front and never put myself again in a position to get spiked or where I couldn't fully expend my energy by the end of the race. My thinking was simple: I didn't want to get trampled or sliced!

This was my first taste of racing against the best runners in the world. I had been beaten, but in the process, based on what I had seen I felt quite certain that if given the opportunity, I was capable of pushing the pace. I calculated that if I improved my fitness, I might even be able to bury the competition with a front-running approach. This might sound arrogant coming from somebody who had yet to reach an Olympic final, but I saw it differently. Just a few weeks before, I wasn't sure if I deserved to be on the same track as the other guys. I had no measuring stick to go by. After two races, I knew everything I did wrong and *still* I was less than a second from qualifying for the semifinal round of the 1500m and six seconds from reaching the steeplechase final. Plus, I wasn't even 20 years old and I had a plan to correct those mistakes.

I don't always have all the answers I want to have, but if there is one thing I know about myself, it's that I am resourceful. If I was to go all in on attacking each race, I had to be willing to sacrifice—enduring the pain it takes to go into oxygen debt in the opening lap of the race and the mental stress it takes to lead the field—and I had to show confidence to push my body and mind to the brink. Otherwise, more committed runners would overtake me.

Embracing the role of pacesetter, as it turned out, would change my life forever.

CHAPTER 6

Changing of the Guard on the Continent

EVERYONE WHO FOLLOWED RUNNING IN THE 1960S AND '70S HAS A favorite memory of Kenya's Kipchoge "Kip" Keino. The one that stands out for me is profound and personal, a display of sportsmanship and kindness that meant a lot more to me than his medals and exceptional racing.

I've made it quite clear how worried I was about getting spiked or knocked down in Munich, and I knew how I could minimize that possibility in the future. But in those opening heats in the 1500m and steeplechase, I had not yet formulated that plan. All I could think of was to run in the second and even third lanes, to avoid contact even when I wasn't in danger of getting boxed in. As anyone who has ever raced anything longer than 400 meters will tell you, the inside lane is the shortest distance to cover—you *always* take the inside lane if you can.

I wasn't willing to take the chance though; I stayed wide. The Kenyan star was in both heats with me, and when I was on the outside, he motioned and called for me to come back in. There he was, a world-famous athlete at work trying to advance to the next round, and he had the presence of mind in the heat of competition to try and help a clueless rookie. That is why I will always respect Keino.

Africa was practically an unknown continent in the athletics world before Keino came on the scene. But if Keino from Kenya opened the floodgates to full blast in changing attitudes, it was Abebe Bikila of Ethiopia who first turned on the spigot. Bikila won the 1960 Olympic marathon running barefoot through the darkening streets of Rome, then became the only repeat gold medalist in the marathon at the 1964 Tokyo Games.

Tokyo was the Olympic debut of Keino, who placed fifth in the 5000m and 10th in the 1500m. In 1966, he took gold in Commonwealth Games record times in both the one-mile and three-mile runs. At the 1968 Olympics, Keino stunned the world. After leading the 10,000m for three laps, he crumpled to the infield with gallstones. Doctors told him not to race anymore during the Games. Instead, just two days later he took silver in the 5000m and qualified for the 1500m final.

On race day for the 1500m final, his bus was stuck in Mexico City traffic, so he hopped off and ran the final two miles to the stadium and checked in just 20 minutes before the start. He then proceeded to dominate the field by almost three seconds, including world record holder Jim Ryun, in an Olympic record time of 3:34.91. Those were the first Games held at altitude, and it led to a surge of interest in training at elevation and the potential of athletes who come from the Rift Valley in East Africa.

I grew up just over the border from Kenya, yet I had no idea who Keino was until the newspapers and radio were talking about his riveting 1968 Olympics breakthrough. Paired with John Stephen Akhwari's inspiring marathon finish in Mexico City, I had two outstanding role models as I made my way onto the running scene in the early 1970s.

The legend of Kip Keino by late 1972 was secure. He followed his two-medal showing in Mexico with another gold-silver combo in Munich. This time he placed second in the 1500m and first in the steeplechase—an event he only entered because the 5000m schedule interfered with the 1500. He had virtually no experience in the steeplechase, and he was not considered as technically skilled as many of the competitors. He stepped on the hurdle most of the time instead of jumping over it. Still, he had beaten me by nearly 14 seconds to advance out of the first heat, and he won the final despite all 23 of the other runners having better personal bests in the steeplechase.

Keino was a global phenomenon. He was an inspiration to me and many others, a role model for success that made us want to follow in his footsteps. During that postcolonial period, when the names, borders, and governments of countries all over the continent were in flux, we weren't all Kenyans, but Keino had forced the world to take notice of a new sphere of influence. That was a source of pride for all Africans.

Looking back, it's hard to overestimate the role he played in introducing the world to the next 50 years of East African distance-running dominance. Keino was the granddaddy of the revolution.

I focused intensely on my training after returning home from a somewhat disappointing Munich Olympics. I was determined not to get boxed in ever again, and that meant deliberate attention to my newly concocted plan.

The East German Werner Kramer offered to help coach me, and I agreed. Erasto Zambi was secretary general of the Tanzania Olympic Committee and the coach of a number of sports at the Kibaha Secondary School outside Dar es Salaam. He was not an experienced distance coach, but with Kramer's help we set up a workout schedule that had me running 100 kilometers (62 miles) a week, and doing intense workouts to build my speed—330-yard intervals and two steep hill sprints, for example, or 6x200m reps.

Fortunately, I was a quick study, and I enjoyed the science of determining the best way to train, the comparison of my results race after race, and the feel of my body working hard and needing recovery. Kramer, Zambi, and Tanzanian head athletics coach Elias Mfungo Sulus were professional and always accommodating to help record my splits and time me, but I soon relied again on developing my own workouts. They were more sophisticated than my personal attempts the year before but attuned to what felt comfortable for me. I would do 15x400 meters with a 200-meter jog after each...so very little rest. Or eight kilometers (five miles) at near race pace for a speed-endurance combination, or 15 sprints of 100 or 200 meters with little rest.

My belief is that for an experienced runner, the coach of the athlete is him- or herself. Once the athlete knows their responsibilities, the coach has nothing much to do rather than overseeing a training program on which they agreed. That is what happened with Kramer, Zambi, and me. If an athlete doesn't see it that way, they will struggle to do the work necessary to achieve greatness. Don't get me wrong though…I'm talking here about elite runners. For young athletes, they definitely need to be guided by a coach who is intelligent about the sport, stays up to date with the latest methods and science, and cares about how to teach effectively. In youth sport, coaches are even more important.

My first test of my new strategy came at the East and Central Africa Championships held at the National Stadium in Dar on December 3, 1972. I bettered my Tanzanian record with a 3:38.9 in my third-ever 1500m, leading start to finish and beating two Kenyans. It was one of the top 10 times in the world that year, but that late in the season, not many took serious notice.

Keino's legacy was not lost on me when it came time for the second All-Africa Games a month later in Lagos, Nigeria. My confidence in my new bold style was high—even with the great Kenyan whom I felt could have been my daddy because of his age and wisdom, and the respect I had for him. Actually, my bigger concern was my own health. Once we arrived, I was shaking and in bed with a temperature over 100 degrees. My muscles and joints ached. I had contracted malaria, likely bitten by a mosquito back in Tanzania several days earlier but only now feeling the virus going through my body.

It wouldn't be the last time malaria created problems for me, but I recovered and flew to sweltering Lagos. In the 1500m heat on January 11, I placed second in 3:48.32, being caught from behind by Ethiopian Olympian Shibrou Regassa and with Keino finishing right behind me in third. I was fine with that performance, and Keino told concerned members of the media that he just wanted to advance to the final.

He remained the fan favorite when we toed the line again on January 13.

I took off from the start and put a good distance between me and the field. Keino pushed me in the final 200 meters, but I held him back and won by two seconds, in 3:37.2—the first time he had ever been beaten on African soil in the 1500m.

This time, with a victory over a legendary Olympic record holder in just the fifth 1500m of my life, I caught people's attention. I was still just 19, but it was as though I had dropped in from another planet.

Journalists from Europe called me "shy" and "quiet" when I answered their questions in English as best as I could.

"If I had been pressed, I think I could have run 3:35," I said. "And the air was so humid, it was difficult to swallow."

Keino himself gave me a vote of confidence and a show of respect—some called it a prophecy and a passing of the torch, since he immediately turned professional with the International Track Association afterward—a day after my win when he was quoted as saying this to a journalist: "If you train hard, you will be the greatest and you will break the world record."

Coach Zambi revealed my malaria attack to the media, adding to the mystique: "Under his fragile appearance, he is very tough," he said. "Also, we both lack experience and have possibly made many errors in training. I have known him only nine months. He trained by himself before."

I was as open and honest about my inexperience as Coach Zambi was. I said I wanted to race in Europe and the United States to learn more. I never claim to have all the answers; I seek them out and then put them into action when I find them. This quote to the reporters after my victory acknowledges that, and really in many ways it sums up my life philosophy in which confidence, commitment, and sacrifice are required to achieve great things:

> I'm not very fast so I must lead all the time and not pay attention to the other runners. But I would like to have someone set a 3:32–33 pace for 1200 meters to see what I could do. I have to experiment to understand many things. Compared to the know-how of the Kenyans, I am

> ignorant...To better my performances, I think I need only to increase the volume of my training and to gain more experience against the best runners. I'm not afraid of anyone, but I can learn from everyone. (Prokop, pgs. 95–96)

It's funny that I suggested using a pacer because this was before pacers—affectionately known as "rabbits"—became common practice in elite track and field. Since I was still relatively unknown at the start of the 1500m final, some commentators actually thought I was a Kenyan employed to push the pace for Keino. Only when I held off his challenge did they realize their mistake.

Pacers were considered inappropriate by many during that era, especially at major international meets. Ben Jipcho sacrificed his own chances for a medal to lead his countryman Keino to his Mexico City breakthrough. Jipcho led Keino through a 56-second opening lap before drifting to the back of the field as Keino built an insurmountable lead. Jipcho later apologized to Ryun for acting as Keino's rabbit.

Just as important as how my signature style changed the way I viewed my competitors, it also changed the way my competitors responded to me. I had turned the tables on them, and this in turn changed the sport. Up to that point in most distance events, it was everybody running in a group waiting for the last 200 meters to sprint it out, then every man for himself. After a few years of me running from the front, pacers started to become a phenomenon. Elite runners conditioned themselves to follow the rabbit, knowing that if the rabbit did his job, they could be in position to compete for a record. This trend became the norm and it helped times to drop more quickly and records to change more frequently. For the time being, though, I was my own rabbit. That is how I wanted it to be if I was going to reach my potential.

I soon began to realize that a calculation I first made simply to keep from getting hurt or hemmed in on the track was actually positioning me to chase world records.

The one being chased from the gun had actually become the aggressor.

//

There have certainly been runners through the years, before and after me, who pushed the pace. That's only common sense. Someone has to be in the lead, and stronger runners have the desire and ability to control the race, wear down the competition, and have enough left at the end to sprint out a victory. I, on the other hand, shot out of the gate looking for an advantage of 20 or 30 meters, which was considered suicidal to most everyone watching. I dared anybody to follow me. If someone got close, I would sprint again to put a gap between us.

Occasionally, I would tire and get caught at the end. Whatever the result, a race with Filbert Bayi was never boring for anyone in attendance.

And as 1973 progressed, I rarely got caught.

My win in Lagos was indeed a springboard to getting invitations to compete in Europe. In 11 races over 40 days that summer, I ran in France (Paris), Sweden (Borås, Stockholm twice, Strängnäs, and Västerås), East Germany (Potsdam), Poland (Warsaw), Denmark (Århus), Norway (Oslo), and Finland (Helsinki). Even in those big capital cities, I was unfazed. Those giant buildings were a new experience compared to Dar and my life as a boy in Karatu, but I was there on business and my office was on the track.

In Helsinki near the end of that stretch, I had a golden opportunity to show the track community my upfront style against some of the very best. I ran the first 100 meters in 12.8 seconds and the first 400 in 53.6. With no one close, I hit my 800- and 1200-meter splits in 1:51.6 and 2:52.2—two seconds ahead of world record pace. I slowed in the late stages but still finished with the world's best time that year in 3:34.6, just 1½ seconds off the historic mark and the third-fastest 1500m ever.

Nearly everyone ran a personal best that day. American Dave Wottle (Olympic gold medalist in the 800) was second in 3:36.2. Jipcho (Olympic silver medalist in the steeplechase) was third in 3:36.6. Steve Prefontaine ran 3:38.1 and placed 11th! As Tom Sturak wrote about me, "A week past his 20th birthday, only nine months after his first serious competition, Bayi had literally run away from the fastest mass-finish 1500m field in history" (Prokop, p. 96).

The very next day, I won the 1500m in Västerås in 3:40.7. It's amazing how often we would race back then. If we were in the vicinity, we raced. If you were successful in one European city, the meet director from another would invite you to an upcoming race in their city with the promise of train fare and a hotel. If you really ran well, you might get to fly to the next destination. There's always a hierarchy. Of course, it's hard to maintain strong performances every time out. The offseason was our chance to rest, I suppose.

Just four days after my win in Helsinki, I competed in the mile for the first time ever on the international stage. My pace at the Dagens Nyheter Galan meet in Stockholm was even faster than my recent 1500m outings, with 52.5 and 1:51 splits for my first two 400s. Midway through the second lap, I led by 75 meters. At 1200 meters, I was still at 2:52 flat. I led through 1500 meters in 3:36.4 before Jipcho ran me down to win in 3:52.0 and I finished at 3:52.86. These were the second- and third-fastest miles in history to date.

Only twice during that 40-day span did I not win. In addition to the DN Galan mile, I placed second at the 800m in Potsdam behind two-time East German Olympian Dieter Fromm in a time of 1:46.9, which set a new Tanzanian record. I won a 1000m race in Paris with an African record time of 2:19.5. The other eight victories were all at 1500m, and five of those I clocked under 3:38.

To show how much I was pushing the pace, Tom Sturak of *Runner's World* logged my fastest and slowest 400, 800, and 1200 splits from those nine races (eight 1500s and one mile). The range was 52.5/56.0, 1:51.0/1:54.0; 2:52.0 (twice)/2:53.5. The 10 fastest 1500m and mile races before 1973 revealed that none of the first or second laps were faster than 55.9 and 1:54.8. The 2:52.5 by Jean Wadoux through 1200 meters when he ran a 3:34.0 1500 was the only comparable split to mine (and Wadoux had pacers in his race).

//

Later that summer, I got to face off against two names that would become familiar to me for years to come. In Tunis, Tunisia, at the African Youth Festival on July 19, I ran a 3:45.3 to beat my fellow Tanzanian Suleiman Nyambui. He is just a few months older than me, and our names would be linked as competitors and teammates numerous times over the next decade.

Five days later, I returned to Oslo, this time for my first visit to the famed Bislett Games to run the 800m. There I faced John Walker of New Zealand for the first time. He beat me by four-hundredths of a second, but my time of 1:46.7 was a Tanzanian record. Every great rivalry must have a starting point. Walker 1, Bayi 0…with many more races to come!

Back in Stockholm the very next day, I took the victory in the 1500m in 3:38.46 while Kenyan Mike Boit beat Walker in the 800.

The only two 1500s that I lost that year came in the fall. I ran a respectable 3:37.85 at the Africa v. USA meet in Dakar, Senegal, but Jipcho ran me down as he had done in the Stockholm mile two months earlier. After winning the 1500m in my first trip to the Western Hemisphere at the Latin America v. Africa meet in Guadalajara, Mexico, I finally got a break in the schedule. When I returned to competition at a 1500m in Nairobi, I turned in 52.0 and 1:52.0 splits, but John Kipkurgat, a veteran 800m specialist from Kenya, managed to slip past me by one-tenth of a second for the victory.

//

From any measure, 1973 was the start of a historic three-year stretch for me. Because of that, the race that started it all—overcoming the Lagos humidity and repulsing Keino's late kick at the start of the season—remains my favorite memory on the track. It opened my eyes to the possibilities.

I was traveling around the world, answering questions about my country, my job, and myself to curious reporters and fans who knew nothing of my background. Many journalists didn't know where or what Tanzania was. I often would just say, "Tanzania is in the south of Kenya."

I had met the greatest living runners, and I'd say I had become one. Just 15 months earlier, I had barely ever left my country and hardly run anything more than a regional race. I didn't understand training or tactics or who the fiercest competitors were...including who was aging and who was ascending.

Now, after a year of running dozens of times at the highest level, I was brimming with confidence, ready to make sure I was the most ascendant runner of them all. I stated clearly when asked that I wanted to beat the world record in the 1500m and win gold at the Commonwealth Games.

My bold (I even have heard it called "anarchic") trademark of not just running from the front but trying to bury my opponents had already dramatically changed my life. It was not a perfect solution; it would require some refining. But more often than not, it got me to the victory stand—and the best was yet to come.

"I thought the only way to avoid spiking was to run from the beginning in front of everybody," I told a CNN reporter years later. "I think I caught some of the athletes with that because they thought I would get tired. They made a bad judgment. They said they'll get me next time, but next time the same thing, and I always say, 'Follow me. Catch me if you can.'"

CHAPTER 7

"The Greatest Race I Have Ever Seen"

THE 10 OTHER 1500M FINALISTS WERE ON THE INFIELD, WARM-UPS concluded, ready to race. I was in the locker room belly of newly built Queen Elizabeth II Park, Christchurch, New Zealand.

When nature calls…

I had tried to pee several times during warm-ups, but I wasn't able to go. Not until race officials at the 1974 Commonwealth Games announced final call for my event did I accept that I had no choice but to take care of business before I could get to work on the track. Rushing downstairs to the mezzanine, I knew I didn't have much time.

There's always lots of frantic energy before a big race, and athletes either try to harness it or find calm in the midst of it. By myself, with all the noise pulsing in the stadium above me, I was fortunate to have removed myself from it and found stillness.

Even though I didn't know a lot of details, I realized the Commonwealth Games were a huge deal back then. This was the 10th edition. Like the Olympics, they occurred every four years and were considered more friendly. With so many countries associated with the faded British Empire, the competition was nearly as good. Highlights at the meet through the years had been epic.

Months after Roger Bannister broke the four-minute barrier in the mile in 1954, he swept past John Landy on the outside in the "mile of the century" as Landy peeked over his inside shoulder on the final turn.

Herb Elliott's 880m and mile combo in '58. Peter Snell doing the same in '62. Kip Keino winning two golds, in the mile and three-mile events, in '66.

Just a week before we lined up for the 1500m final in Christchurch, New Zealander Dick Tayler had thrilled the hometown crowd with a win in the 10,000m on the opening night of competition. The victory seemed to electrify the entire meet, especially since it was the first time a summer sports event could be seen on color TV in New Zealand. While Tayler's win had come in front of some empty seats, here on the last race of the meet, the stadium—built specifically for the Commonwealth Games—was packed. It was our turn to close it with a bang.

My bladder was clearly feeling anxiety, but my brain knew full well how strong my training had been for this moment. Despite a fantastic 1973, I was still not the main guy on people's radars. Earlier in these Games, I had placed fourth in the 800m, behind two others who were also in the 1500m field: Kenyan Mike Boit had taken silver and New Zealand's own John Walker had earned bronze.

Walker's elder countryman Rod Dixon had taken third in the 1500m less than two years ago in the Olympics and the crowd would be rooting hard for him as well. Ben Jipcho was a silver medalist in the steeplechase in Munich and had been running at a high level for years with the great Keino. Already in Christchurch he had won gold in the 5000m and steeplechase, so he was going for a rare triple gold. Brendan Foster was bronze medalist at the 1970 Commonwealth Games in this event.

I was a gimmick, that guy who ran from the front and hung on as long as he could.

As I rushed back upstairs (a little lighter and a lot relieved) and saw the open sky, I felt the vibrations of the bleachers give way to cheers filling my ears and the breeze on my face. I was ready for whatever my opponents had in store.

I may have only been 20 years old, but I knew that perception was not reality. My front-running was no gimmick; it was a calculated strategy I was more than prepared to execute.

//

There was plenty of buzz about whether I would push the pace so hard against the very best middle-distance runners. That strategy might work in lesser meets, the theory went, where you could wear down the field, but you can't run away from Jipcho, Dixon, Boit, and Walker. Walker and Dixon didn't know me well yet, and I believe they thought they would run me down. In fact, Walker had already done just that to take the bronze from me at the much shorter 800m distance. Jipcho had done it twice the year before. But with my recent training for the 1500m, I was confident that anyone trying to close the gap over the last 100 or 200 meters would have a real fight on their hands.

Foster was later quoted about discussions among the runners: "Before the race, there was plenty of chatter," Foster said. "We all knew what the guy was going to do and because it was the Commonwealth Games everyone could speak English. 'My God, he's going to go out and he's probably going to go out earlier than we think,' I said. My compatriot, John Kirkbride, said, 'Are you going to go with him? It's a stupid way to run a 1500m race.' I said, 'John, we've got no choice'" (*New Zealand Herald*, 2014).

I felt like an underdog. Keith Quinn, race commentator for TV New Zealand, had written a preview of the race for a weekly national news magazine called *The Listener*. An editor changed my name to Gilbert Bayi, reasoning that nobody would have a name like Filbert.

I had no doubt about what I would do. When the gun sounded, I rushed to the front and forced them to chase me. I put some 10 meters between me and the field. That was a huge gap for a 1500m race, which back then often would start cautiously. My first 300 meters was 40.6 seconds, five seconds faster than Jim Ryun ran to open his world record from 1967. My first 400 meters was 54.9, which was actually a bit slow for me compared to my 1500s the previous summer.

Still, after the first lap, I knew something special was happening. I felt sure I would win gold or improve my previous best time over 1500m, maybe even have a shot at Ryun's record. As when I beat Keino in Lagos, it was all going according to my plan.

But none of the others panicked. They stayed in a group, within striking distance, figuring that strength in numbers would carry at least some of them past me before the finish line.

I extended my lead to about 20 meters by the 800-meter mark in 1:52.2. At the bell lap (1200 meters), I clocked a 2:50.8—faster than I had ever gotten there in my one previous mile and many 1500s.

We didn't have a giant video board like runners do today. So that's when I peeked over my shoulder and thought they were making up ground. Their presence was no surprise to me, and I had done enough speed training to know I could accelerate some more and still be able to push in the last 200 meters if I needed to. I know this sounds too simple, but this was unfolding just as I wanted it to. I had full confidence in my plan and the training I had done to put it into action.

It was interesting later to find out how much the other runners said they actually liked the hot pace. They felt good and thought they were in position to assert themselves when necessary, but this is where the hunters miscalculated. Instead of finding strength in numbers, they had to fight off one another. They had to make space for themselves as they lengthened their strides for the sprint. Most immediately, they had to read each other and determine who was going to make the decision to move.

With 400 meters to go, Dixon did.

"There was nobody else prepared to go after him," Dixon said later. "We were coming up with a lap to go and I had to take over. I thought, 'I'm going to run this last 400 as hard as I can. I'm not going to sit around and wait for a sprint. I have to go out'" (*New Zealand Herald*, 2014).

Jipcho led Walker past Dixon on the backstretch. When Jipcho slowed, Walker knew time was running short, and he overtook Jipcho on the final curve. I took another quick look back and saw that Walker was gaining on me as we neared the homestretch. Instead of feeling desperate,

Holding off John Walker and Ben Jipcho for a world record in the 1500m, this finish at the 1974 Commonwealth Games in Christchurch became my introduction to the world.

I actually relaxed my muscles and stayed in continuous rhythm every step—a fluid contrast to the hard-charging Walker, who must have had two inches of height and 45 pounds on me.

On the final straightaway, I looked back again. I did not have a reputation as a strong kicker, but I knew then I would win the race. I set my engine into its final gear. Walker closed to within two steps of me over the last 50 meters. I looked back twice, but he could not overtake me. He looked disappointed at the finish, arms outreached, head back, knowing he was too late. Walker, an 800m specialist, had waited too long to move.

Ben Jipcho (left) of Kenya and my Tanzanian countryman, Suleiman Nyambui (right), congratulate me after my world record on February 2, 1974.

I broke the tape and looked at the clock. The information was displayed clearly for all to see, and immediately I grasped what I had done.

My 3:32.2 was the equivalent of a 3:49.2 mile, a time that would have shattered the existing world record by almost two seconds. I made my way around to the backstretch, ecstatic, hopping up and down as though I still had another lap's worth of energy in me. I lifted my arms to the sellout crowd of 25,000 in the brand-new stadium—all of them standing, including Her Majesty, the namesake of the stadium. Walker caught up to congratulate me. We hugged and smiled. With a 3:32.5, he too had broken Ryun's mark. I took his hand so he could join me on the rest of my lap.

1500 FINAL MEN

WR: 3:33.1 *CR:* 3:36.6

1. Bayi	TANZANIA	3.32.2
2. Walker	NEW ZEALAND	3.32.5
3. Jipcho	KENYA	3.33.2

"I was absolutely ecstatic, delighted," Walker said later. "I said to Filbert, 'You've broken the world record,' and he said, 'So have you!' He wanted me to do a victory lap with him and I said, 'No, it's your time. You have broken the world record.' He insisted and I felt a bit embarrassed" (*New Zealand Herald*, 2014).

I was proud to have Walker join me for the rest of the victory lap in front of his home crowd. Near the steeplechase water pit, Jipcho and my fellow Tanzanian Suleiman Nyambui caught up to me, having jogged counterclockwise back across the homestretch. The three of us hugged each other and they congratulated me.

New Zealand is a country with a rich distance-running tradition. Their cheers felt authentic. They loved their guys, who had finished second and fourth, but the fans knew they had witnessed something special. They were celebrating what the entire field had done.

The performances from the other runners were also remarkable. Five new national records were set. Five of us (me, Walker, Jipcho, Dixon, and Graham Crouch of Australia) broke the Commonwealth Games record. Ralph King of the *New Zealand Herald* called it "the most glorious metric mile in history." No less an authority than Sir Roger

Bannister called it "the greatest race I have ever seen." As the famed BBC athletics commentator David Coleman put it, looking back, "It had been the fastest, and undoubtedly the bravest, 1500m race the world had ever seen."

Jipcho held off Dixon for third place in 3:33.2, salvaging bronze to go with his two gold medals at the meet. Dixon's time of 3:33.9 was the fifth-fastest 1500m in history—but on this day it wasn't even good enough for a medal: "I stood there in total amazement," Dixon recalled. "I walked off the track and someone called to me, 'Loser.' I thought, 'Shit, come on, I ran the fifth-fastest time in history. I know I finished fourth but was only three steps away from winning. How can I be a loser?' In fourth place you don't get any prizes" *(New Zealand Herald, 2014).*

//

That's what pushing the pace will do, and I'll happily take the credit. It probably sounds like I'm lacking humility to talk like that. I don't mean to sound arrogant, but I've said many times through the years how I feel like the changes I implemented through this bold strategy have been forgotten. People forget how much pacing was frowned upon back then—remember Jipcho apologizing for leading Keino to victory?

In a 2004 articlé in *The Guardian* on the eve of the 50th anniversary of Bannister's first four-minute mile, Pat Butcher wrote that the pacing, overt and covert, that marked the groundbreaking feat had ruined middle-distance racing. Though pacing was considered unacceptable, it was practiced and occasionally condoned for decades before it became commonplace (and lucrative) in the late 1970s and 1980s. Butcher disapproved…strongly:

> The defining moment of 20th-century middle-distance running didn't occur in Oxford on May 6 1954; it came in the Queen Elizabeth II stadium in Christchurch, New Zealand, on February 2 1974. And the

genius to whom we should all be paying homage is not Roger Bannister but Filbert Bayi of Tanzania.

When Bayi dared to run away from the field in the Commonwealth Games 1,500m final in 1974, he set an example for the event that has done so much to define international athletics throughout the century-and-a-half of organised running. Bayi opened with a lap of 54.9sec, and just kept going. New Zealand's John Walker was catching Bayi throughout the last lap, and was barely a metre behind on the final bend. In those circumstances, 99 times out of 100, the pursuer bursts past to victory. But with barely a backward glance, Bayi stretched away again. He won in 3min 32.2sec, breaking the world record by 0.9sec. And he had run every step of the way in front. That is class.

My first appearance on the cover of *Track & Field News*, March 1974.

> Bayi's performance is an indictment of every middle-distance runner who thinks that they have to be paced to turn in a decent time. The film of his run should be compulsory viewing for every aspiring middle-distance runner. Unfortunately, all they'll be seeing this week will be reruns of that flickering film of three white-vested establishment figures visiting another British sporting disaster on the world.

In effect, I regularly chose to be the rabbit most of the time I was in a final in the mid-1970s. There was, however, a big difference between me and the rabbits who within just a few years were getting paid good money to set the pace: I didn't drop out after three laps; I won.

In the process, I forced elite runners to up their game. Times were lowered, records were broken, and expectations were raised.

Before the 2014 Commonwealth Games in Glasgow, Scotland, in recognition of my achievement that 40 years later still stood as the meet record, I was interviewed by Hugh MacDonald of the *Glasgow Herald*:

> Bayi…is slightly mystified—even miffed—at the way his Christchurch achievement has been treated in the history of athletics.
>
> "It has been forgotten," he says without anger. "People never talk about Filbert Bayi. There must be something wrong with this athletics family because a lot of people have been inducted in the hall of fame by the IAAF but Filbert Bayi has never been mentioned. I do not know why.
>
> "Think about the change that occurred in the 1500m at Christchurch. The 1500m was usually a slow race and then a sprint [at the finish]. But in 1974 I changed that from the beginning to the end. And not many people have thought about that."
>
> Bayi set off quickly and, at 800m, was 20m clear of a class field. He points out that previous and many subsequent 1500m world records have been set with the help of pacemakers. "The person who wins the race is behind watching," he points out. "They are assisted by others. I do not believe that is a real world record. The world record is when somebody uses all his effort and does it by himself."

> So does he feel that his achievement has not been properly recognised? "Definitely, 100%. It is only now that people are realising what happened. It is now almost exactly 40 years on and I am being interviewed by people in Australia, UK and New Zealand."
>
> He recalls the finish precisely, noting the positions of Jipcho and Walker when they launched their desperate challenges for gold. "I looked back and saw people coming. And then I waited. And then John Walker came close to me—about three metres away—at 50 metres and then I just accelerated. I saw the finish line and thought, Nobody will catch me."
>
> And nobody did. (MacDonald, 2014)

I thought Foster, who placed seventh in a British national record of 3:37.64, said it well when he looked back 40 years later on my historic day of February 2, 1974:

> Nobody could live with Filbert. He was at the limit of human endeavour at that time. In those days we didn't have pacemakers. Filbert was a fantastic pacemaker, but he just kept going. He was changing the rules. People only broke world records when they had pacemakers. The pacemaker broke the world record that day. It was a new era in distance running...The great thing was that Jipcho, Walker and Dixon were even able to compete with him. The New Zealand crowd saw what I believe, apart from the first four-minute mile, the most significant mile/1500m race in history. When you look back on it, it is still a wonderful performance by Filbert Bayi. There wasn't a human being living who could have got anywhere near that. That was his moment. (*New Zealand Herald*, 2014)

//

No question the Commonwealth Games was my moment, at least up until that point in my life.

Being underestimated by other runners or going into a race unnoticed was no longer an option. The world knew me now. Becoming the first African to hold the 1500m world record will do that. I had enjoyed being the underdog, but I also knew the best chance I had to be a great runner was to race against the best. And now I was one of the first to be invited to the biggest races in Europe that summer.

I started this book when the bell lap sounded in Christchurch: "The next 55.4 seconds will transform my life," I wrote. And it did.

It certainly didn't make me rich, not in those days of amateur athletics. Being noticed does have other advantages though, and my life was further transformed four months later when I competed in the Eastern Africa Army Games at the University of Dar es Salaam. I won the 800m and the 1500m, but the significance of that meet had nothing to do with my performance on the track.

After we finished our races, athletes had to report to the secretariat. I walked into the tent where a slim, young woman with long hair was

With the Tanzanian Army athletics squad before competing in the 1974 Eastern Africa Army Games held at the University of Dar es Salaam Sports Courts. I'm kneeling, in the middle of the front row wearing an adidas sweatsuit. This was just a few days before I met the love of my life.

typing results. I'm not a romantic guy and it sounds like a storybook for me to say it, but as soon as our eyes met, I knew I had found the person I wanted to spend my life with.

Anna Lyimo seemed to feel the same way when she looked up from her work as a meet official. We hadn't even spoken to each other yet, but it seemed we were already listening to each other. If you could see into our hearts and minds, you could see that we "got" each other right away.

Soon we were dating, though I was nervous when I came to see her. Anna was living with her sister and her husband, who was a policeman. They lived at police headquarters, and I had to ask her sister for permission to take her out. I assure you, I brought her home immediately after going to a movie. If I said Anna would be back by 8 p.m., we were there by 7:55!

We were a good combination from the start, and we greatly respected each other. She was hardworking, caring, and one of the smartest people I knew. Like me, she was Christian, though she was Lutheran and I was

Catholic. I honestly don't know when I first told her that I loved her or she told me that she loved me, but it was clear from our actions and words from the start. I do know that she enjoyed taking care of her flowers and it wasn't long before I gave her a red rose as my first gift to her.

I lived at the army base, and the police station was close to the national stadium, about eight kilometers (five miles) away. Anna had just moved to Dar from Same District in the Kilimanjaro Region, following her sister to the big city when her brother-in-law became a police officer. Same is about 350 kilometers (215 miles) from where I grew up in Karatu.

Anna was a netball player in local tournaments, so she was knowledgeable and skilled at sports, but she said she applied for the sports council job mostly because it was close to the police headquarters.

She certainly knew I was a world record holder, but she didn't make a fuss over it. I always felt like Christchurch made it that much more likely that I would meet her because my success gave the national sports council more work to do, though surely it was our destiny to meet anyway.

At that time, my sole focuses were training for races and my air transport work in the army. Dating was a waste of time, I told myself. But when you see someone as beautiful as Anna, you definitely don't have any option.

Truly, Anna was my first love, and I was certain we would stay together forever and ever.

My days of not considering myself a romantic were over. Running was no longer my heart's only partner.

1974 COMMONWEALTH GAMES

Queen Elizabeth II Park, Christchurch, New Zealand

February 2, 1974

1500m Final

1.	Filbert Bayi	TANZANIA	3:32.16*	WR
2.	John Walker	NEW ZEALAND	3:32.52	NR
3.	Ben Jipcho	KENYA	3:33.16	NR
4.	Rod Dixon	NEW ZEALAND	3:33.89	
5.	Graham Crouch	AUSTRALIA	3:34.22	NR
6.	Mike Boit	KENYA	3:36.84	
7.	Brendan Foster	ENGLAND	3:37.64	NR
8.	Suleiman Nyambui	TANZANIA	3:39.62	
9.	David Fitzsimons	AUSTRALIA	3:41.30	
10.	John Kirkbride	ENGLAND	3:41.91	
11.	Randal Markey	AUSTRALIA	3:44.56	
DNS	Tony Polhill	NEW ZEALAND		

**The Commonwealth Games first used fully automatic timing in 1974 and my time was 3:32.16. But in the days before fully automatic timing was the norm, all times recorded in hundredths of a second were rounded up to the next tenth. My world record was ratified as 3:32.2, as shown on the plaque (right) that I received from the IAAF months later. World records were not recorded in hundredths of a second until 1981.*

CHAPTER 8

The Return of John Walker

JOHN WALKER IS A GRACIOUS MAN. IN MY OPINION, HIS COACH, ARCH Jelley, gave him bad advice prior to the Commonwealth Games' 1500m final. Jelley questioned my frontrunning strategy and led Walker to believe I would not have the speed to withstand his charge in the final 200 meters, no matter how far ahead I might be. I don't believe Jelley was even convinced I would use that approach in a major final. Furthermore, he had Walker wait for someone else (it turned out to be Rod Dixon) to move on the final lap.

Walker had not proven himself in the 1500m yet—his best was 3:38 before he ran 3:32.52 behind my world record for the second-fastest time ever—so perhaps the caution was understandable. But you know my view on caution in distance running...and you see where caution got the guys who chased me that day in Christchurch in 1974.

"I wasted too much energy trying to catch him," Walker said when interviewed decades later. "By the time I got to the straight, it looked like I was catching him but I wasn't. He was still holding me the whole way. I was tying up at 90 meters. He never slowed down. He won that race. Not me. He didn't die. If I had got up to him, he might have faltered because there's a big difference when there's pressure on—but he never died" (*New Zealand Herald*, 2014).

At a World Athletics celebration in 2019, Walker told the crowd, including me and many middle-distance greats from the past half-century,

"I've looked at the video over the years. Filbert ran an extraordinary race. I was coming from behind but I was never going to catch him. He went straight out from the gun and went to the front and broke the world record. That was never heard of in European racing. So—well done, my friend" (Rowbottom, 2019).

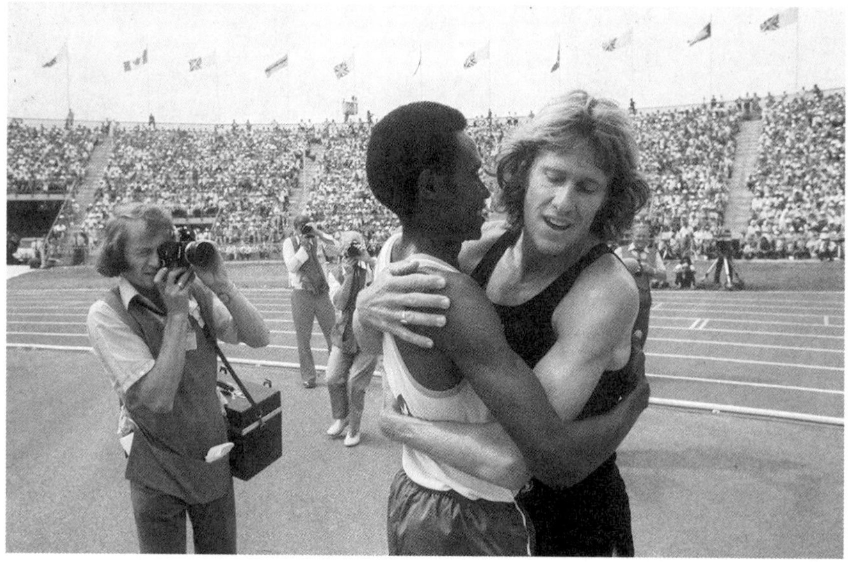

My friend John Walker immediately congratulated me after my 1974 world record in the 1500m in his home country of New Zealand.

Sports is built on great rivalries, and I maintain that individual real-time rivalries are more compelling than those of team v. team. Fans are drawn to contrasting styles and personalities, gauging how the two get along in and out of competition, debating who is better. This is not a question of who is the GOAT (Greatest of All Time); it's a discussion about the better of two greats *in head-to-head competition*. El Guerrouj/Morceli. McEnroe/Borg. Gebrselassie/Tergat. Nicklaus/Palmer. Coe/Ovett. Navratilova/Evert. Federer/Nadal. Graf/Seles. Woods/Mickelson.

By any measure, John Walker and I were great rivals. I believe we did honor to our sport in how we approached our battles and spoke about each other. Though we had faced off in Oslo once in 1973, Christchurch in 1974 was the real beginning of our friendship. He kept me from receiving a bronze medal in the 800m and he earned another medal, a silver, in the 1500. But I was now the 1500m world record holder—which I would say gave me the advantage!

//

With both of us in high demand after the Commonwealth Games, it didn't take long for us to meet again. Even if we didn't say so directly to each other, I think he and I both sensed that our time to achieve great things was now, and we were more likely to get an education by battling each other every opportunity we got.

Back in Helsinki in June, where a year earlier in the 1500m I had claimed my first major European victory, I was running faster than ever, with splits of 52.9, 1:50.4, and 2:50.4. That was faster than I had run in Christchurch or the previous year at the Helsinki Olympic Stadium. Walker was six seconds back just beyond the halfway point, but he cruised over the final 300 meters to easily win in 3:33.89. I took silver with a pedestrian time of 3:37.20 in a field that included Dixon and Crouch from the Christchurch record-setting race, plus Thomas Wessinghage of West Germany and Bronisław Malinowski, a young Polish steeplechasing star who placed fourth in Munich.

I wasn't surprised that I struggled, as I had been doing shorter speedwork, rarely beyond 1200 meters. I pushed hard anyway, and all credit to Walker for learning, making the adjustment, and beating me. He clearly stated that he thought he could have beaten me in Christchurch if he had gone after me earlier. In Helsinki, Walker did just that and proved his point.

Through the years, Walker, Dixon, and I saw each other often on the racing circuit. We would occasionally join each other for training runs. In Oslo, I turned around early on a workout with them once. Dixon told me later that Walker thought I was rude to just peel off during a 90-minute run. "John," Dixon reassured him, "he's got a schedule to keep just like you do."

Dixon was the most talkative of the three of us, which didn't always help with communication! They talked fast in their New Zealand accents and lingo, and I just tried to keep up with the conversation. When I spoke English in my Tanzanian accent, they didn't know what I was saying half the time either. But Dixon told me one time how his mother was the most influential person in his life, and she told him to always look people in the eye. "You've got to tell them you like and love them even if you don't speak the same language," he said, repeating his mother's wise words.

They liked to stay out later than I did, and Walker and I weren't always in the mood to say much, but I can say without a doubt that there was always respect and honor from day one forward with those guys. It became clear in words and action for decades to come.

Helsinki was the start of a stretch of five races in eight days in Scandinavia. In Västerås, Sweden, the next day, I won the 800m in 1:47.1. The field included Robert Ouko, who had been on Kenyan gold-medal-winning relay teams at the 1970 Commonwealth Games and the 1972 Olympics.

I hate to admit it, but chatter from running journalists influenced me to experiment with different tactics. In a mile at the DN Galan meet in Stockholm on July 1, I ran opening laps of just 57 and 58 seconds, but won in 3:54.1. In the 1500m the next day, I stayed in the pack until sprinting the final 300 meters to win in 3:43.16. But I found the slow pace tiring. I felt like I wouldn't have been any more exhausted if I had run a 1:52 opening 800 meters than the 1:57 that I did run. I declared that I was done experimenting.

On the off day between Stockholm and the Bislett Games in Oslo, Norway, the media following the sport didn't let me off the hook. They liked the fact that I was trying a more conventional approach and said it would pay dividends. I had a couple of them explain to me—the world-record holder, you understand!—exactly how they thought a person should successfully run a 1500.

A bit annoyed by that point, I claimed the 800m was now my favorite race and I would run it in Oslo. Walker returned from a brief stint in Italy, where he had won the 1500m in Milan. We were at the same place again, but in two different races—with two very different results. While Walker won the 3000m, race organizers begged me to reconsider and run the 1500m so that the fans wouldn't be disappointed in seeing me at my world-record distance. I agreed, but decided I would keep experimenting with staying in the pack and then sprinting to the finish.

Near the end of the third lap, I regretted my decision. Mike Boit ran into me from behind, and the spikes on my right shoe cut my left knee as I fell. The DNF was the least of my concerns; 12 stitches would sideline me indefinitely.

It takes a lot for me to get mad. Even if I'm not happy, I don't generally voice my frustration. I'll stay quiet. This time though…man, I was furious, and after snapping at an Italian writer, I decided to talk to the media less. "It's all you journalists' fault!" I yelled at him. "If it hadn't been for you, I never would have run that way!" (Prokop, pgs. 97–8).

I was surely too harsh to blame them for my decision, but sometimes I felt I had to be gruff with the journalists or they would try to get in my brain. I understood they needed to fulfill their requirements, but I just wanted to rest and avoid them. I didn't care about being advertised. That was not for me. I ran for pride and pleasure, not for money.

//

The U-shaped scar on my left knee marked me for years, and I decided again that I would always run from the front. "Never again in the group," I said. "I will train harder so I can start faster and maybe set a 1:49 pace. I am working on it" (Prokop, p. 98).

I was out for a month with my injured knee, a forced layoff that cost me the rest of the summer schedule. Then I was off for a three-month army officer's training course. In December, after just two weeks of training, I easily won Tanzanian national championships in the 800m (1:49) and 1500m (3:44). I mostly competed just to shake off the rust and out of appreciation for my fans in our home country.

Soon after the calendar turned to 1975, I received the 1974 African Athlete of the Year award in Zaire from President Mobutu Sese Seko. This was just over two months after the "Rumble in the Jungle" between Muhammad Ali and George Foreman turned the world's attention to the country.

Then I made a triumphant return to Christchurch. I was more than happy to accept an invitation for the New Zealand Games, where my breakthrough had occurred almost exactly a year earlier. I ran a 3000m time trial in 7:53.9, then beat Walker by four-tenths of a second in my second-best 800m to date, 1:45.5—I had actually run 1:45.32 when I placed fourth in the Commonwealth Games. Walker turned the tables on me in Auckland four days later with a 1:46.7 in the 800m, beating me by six-tenths of a second. John Kipkurgat, the 800m gold medalist in the 1974 Commonwealth Games, placed third both times.

"Filbert is a New Zealand hero," Walker said recently. "There has never been another athlete like him. He had so much courage and ability, a true champion."

As I said, John Walker is a gracious man.

My next chance at a whole slew of great runners, including some new faces and some old, would come on a new type of stage in the media capital of the world.

CHAPTER 9

No Mickey-Mousing Around

I HAD CLEARLY STATED MY DESIRE TO TALK LESS TO JOURNALISTS AFTER my injury in Oslo. That soon turned out to be problematic because I was headed to New York City and my first trip to the strange, media-saturated United States.

In three days, I was set to run at storied Madison Square Garden in my first-ever indoor race. The Wanamaker Mile—the showcase event of the Millrose Games—was the start of a month-long, five-race, coast-to-coast-to-coast tour. We stayed in Princeton, New Jersey, outside the city when we arrived. As I understood it, Princeton University coach Larry Ellis, the first African-American coach in any sport in America's prestigious Ivy League, had arranged it since he had connections with coaches in Africa.

This suited me because it gave me a short break outside the limelight before I would be surrounded by reporters. The first morning, we were met by a Princeton runner.

"Hi," our host said. "I'm Craig Masback."

Suleiman Nyambui was there. So was Claver Kamanya, a sprinter who was the Tanzanian flag-bearer at the 1972 Olympics, and the head of our delegation, Protase Muchwampaka.

Masback tells the rest of the story:

> At practice one day, Larry Ellis said a group of Tanzanian athletes were going to train here the next few days, including Filbert Bayi. My roommates and I were huge fans of the sport. We'd followed his story. The idea that a world record holder would be training at our facilities was super exciting. I went up to Larry afterward and said, "We'd love to show them the local runs. We run on these streets and paths every day and we'd love to run with them."
>
> He said to meet them at 5 o'clock. I said, "But it's winter. It gets dark at 4." "No," Larry said. "5 a.m.!" I wasn't going to turn that down. I'll never forget: they each had three sweatsuits on, the old cotton variety. I'm of course exaggerating. But they were layered up. Basically everybody but Filbert had decided it was too cold to run outside. They went to our indoor track and Larry must have opened it up for them. I went with Filbert outdoors. It was kind of a life-changing experience for me. That was my sophomore year. That year we won the NCAA indoor two-mile relay. We had OK runners, but there was a saying on our team, "If you're running too fast to talk, you're running too fast." Most guys were concerned about how many miles, not the pace.
>
> So, the moment had come. Filbert and I are doing the run together. He takes off. I'm not exaggerating, it had to be five-minute pace, probably 5:15 or 5:30. Later in my career, that's what I trained at, but I had never seen it. Theoretically, I was leading him on a run, but just enough to keep him in sight. I was putting turns in to give me any chance of slowing him down. It was probably the hardest of any run I had ever been on. There was no conversation, let's put it that way.
>
> The next morning I come back to run with him again, but I'm told that Filbert had already left. "Too many turns," someone said. "He couldn't get into the flow."

I didn't remember that incident myself, but it was the first of many times that I've seen Craig through the years. He became one of the top milers in the world soon after that, and later an NBC sports commentator, CEO of USA Track and Field, and marketing executive at Nike. He's always been gracious and humble to me, curious to know how I am doing.

I'll give him credit for his work as a running guide in cold Princeton. Once indoors, I managed a new meet record of 3:59.3 in the Wanamaker Mile. I ran with the group and nipped two college stars at the end: Paul Cummings of Brigham Young (3:59.6) and Wilson Waigwa of the University of Texas-El Paso (4:00.2). A distant fourth was a local star and former Olympian, Marty Liquori. Waigwa was a 25-year-old Kenyan who was in his first year at UTEP. He was the first of many African distance runners that coach Ted Banks brought in who led the Miners' domination of NCAA cross country and track and field over the next decade.

//

This was my first time to run indoors, and that created its own intrigue for reporters. They wondered if I would be able to win when I wasn't running from the front. No question about it, indoor racing required new considerations. "I think it is time I changed my tactics. I can't use the old ones indoors," I told Ron Reid of *Sports Illustrated*. "My goal now is not a world record, but to learn to run indoors. People think that I must always go to the front, but I don't now like to lead all the way… They would like me to run ahead, but I have to save my strength for the end. They are more experienced. I don't know indoors and I am just using this for training."

The tight turns on a 160-meter oval made it impossible to open a gap on the field the way I did outdoors. In addition, the interlocking banked boards that make up the track slow you down. They absorb your strides, as though you're sinking into them. The incessant pounding of footsteps sounded like a construction site, or perhaps cattle loping over the range.

I didn't like the air conditioning either. I found it difficult to take deep breaths of oxygen under such conditions, even more so than in the humidity of Dar or Lagos. The air in those cities was stifling, but at least it was natural. In Los Angeles, I warmed up for two hours—90 minutes fast and 30 minutes of jogging—because I was so cold inside the Forum. In a hot outdoor race, I only needed an hour for warm-up.

The reporters also wanted to know where I grew up, how I trained, and what Tanzania was like. These were the same questions I had already tired of in Europe, asked all over again and more aggressively. Looking back at some of those interviews, I can see why I was considered "diffident, a mystery." I was 21 years old and still quite new at speaking English. With so much travel throughout January already and a February full of flying from New York to California and back to New York, I tried to rest whenever I wasn't training or racing, so I wasn't very patient.

When asked about whether running was painful, I said, "It is just like walking, as God made you."

With so much new thrown at me, I was also naïve. At the Los Angeles Times Indoor Games, meet director Will Kern asked me if I wanted to go to Disneyland while I was in town. I had no idea what he was talking about.

"Of all the athletes we've brought here from all over the world, including the Soviet Union, in the 16 years of the Times Games, Bayi is the only one who never heard of Mickey Mouse and Disneyland," Kern said. "Did you ever try to explain Mickey Mouse to somebody who never heard of him?" (Jordan, p. 9).

I wasn't in the United States to learn about a cartoon or ride rollercoasters anyway. I took my racing seriously, and the indoor tour was an opportunity to race against new guys in a new format. Above all, this tour was a chance for me to learn and, I suppose, a chance for others to learn about me. Tom Sturak of *Runner's World* wrote a book chapter on me:

> I spent considerable time with Bayi while he was on the West Coast. I found him to be shy and reserved, often seemingly moody and aloof. By the time we met in Los Angeles (his first race on the tour had been in New York), he had obviously grown weary of running an endless

> gauntlet of newsmen. However, he allowed me two lengthy interviews; and I was able to observe him up close both at rest and in training over a week's period. I also established a rapport with two of his teammates, Capt. Protase Muchwampaka and Claver Kamanya; and I talked about Bayi with his good friend and chief rival John Walker of New Zealand. In addition, I read everything on Bayi that I could find.
>
> Off the track and on, however, Filbert Bayi has an elusive character. He impresses me as being an extremely intelligent, sensitive, complex and driven young man; but I do not claim to know him. (Prokop, pp. 94–5)

Even if journalists still didn't know what to make of me, performance-wise and education-wise, my first American journey was a success. They could call me a loner and say I was morose; all I know is that when I got ready to train or race, I was transformed. I'd get chatty with my training partners, and a slight smile would come across my face. From the time I was a young boy, running has always been able to take me to that place.

//

The LA Times meet brought a capacity crowd of 16,400 to the Forum in Inglewood, California. It was a five-man field that included American fan favorite Steve Prefontaine, Walker, Dixon, and Byron Dyce, who unlike the rest of us had years of experience in indoor racing.

I let Prefontaine take the lead just one lap in and settled into second place through the first half of the mile race. Walker lurked just behind me in the lineup as the crowd's murmuring turned into a continuous din. They were ready for somebody to move. Walker and I slid into the lead by the three-quarter mark in 3:02.6. With two laps to go, Pre made a slight push, but we held off that challenge rather easily. Walker was anxious to take charge, but I held him off with a consistent, smooth stride in the tight quarters and forced him to stay almost in the second lane until the end. My 3:59.6 was nearly identical to my Wanamaker Mile and three-tenths of a second ahead of Walker.

Even indoors and not exploding to an early lead, I carried out a similar approach over the final laps. When Walker was just off my shoulder, I would sneak glances on the curves—which never seemed to stop coming—and relax as I slightly accelerated to a 57.3-second final 440 yards. People said I finished fresh, as though I didn't struggle.

When Tom Jordan asked if the win was "easy" for me, I replied in a way that sounds cryptic but then turns into a pretty standard racing explanation that anybody over the past century might have given:

> I feel that there is no easy race. It just happens somebody wins and when that happens, the crowd says it looked like an easy race. I wasn't tired yesterday in the race because I wasn't running very fast.
>
> Most of the time, I am running fast for the first two laps but yesterday I was just relaxing for the first two, because when you run with experienced athletes, you must be very careful; you must keep them in front, not behind. That is why I let Prefontaine pass me, to go ahead. I let him until they slow the speed. Everybody wanted not to lead the way, you see. (Jordan, p. 9)

//

Next stop a week later was down the Pacific Coast in San Diego. Just as I had passed on the movie studio tour in LA, now I passed on the trip to the San Diego Zoo. Why would I want to go to a zoo? I grew up next door to the Serengeti and Ngorongogo Crater. My country is filled with more animals than a human could ever see in a lifetime!

The anticipation at the Jack in the Box Games at the San Diego Sports Arena was immense. Our race was being billed as the "Greatest Indoor Mile in History." It included not just Walker and me, but Rick Wohlhuter, an American with a reputation as being a great indoor racer over the previous five years. Adding to the excitement, another American, Francie Larrieu, broke the world indoor mile record for women with a 4:29.0 just before our race. Reporters even called her "Filberta," but she deserves to keep her own name.

The track was laid over an ice hockey rink and it was cold in there, but I did an extended warm-up to prepare. I waited longer to get to the infield than the rest of the field, making them wait while I put on my Puma spikes.

When the gun sounded, a runner named Ed Zuck took off and led us through a 54.5 opening quarter and still led at the halfway mark. I took the lead with a plodding third quarter, then with a 55-second final quarter held off a hard-charging Walker for the second week in a row by half a second. My time of 3:56.4 tied for the third-fastest indoor mile ever, but what made me happy was how I did it. I let a non-favorite lead, then I slowed the pace before showing a kick that people still maintained I did not have. What I didn't realize is that Zuck had been hired by the race promoter as a pacer. He got up 10 yards on me before I started to reel him in.

Sturak was impressed:

> More interesting (if not such "good copy") was the slow third quarter (63.4, Bayi leading), that lost the fans a world record but won him a brilliant tactical battle. Watching Bayi one might have noted nothing more than the fact he often looked behind when coming out of the turns—and that he stayed in front. But what was happening with Wohlhuter told the whole story. Never more than a tick behind through three-quarters, he was the natural favorite—an experienced, proven first-class indoor runner with a long string of victories on the boards. Yet running behind Bayi's varying tempo, Wohlhuter appeared an awkward novice, often left hanging up on a curve, once running into Bayi's spikes, looking more tense and less threatening with every passing lap.
>
> Afterwards, Wohlhuter, visibly dazed, rationalized that he was not used to 'running this kind of (slow) tempo…I'd get bogged down, start running to catch up, then have to slow again.' In other words, Bayi had played with the pace and with him. As Walker (well-versed in Bayi's tactics) explained later: 'Bayi runs where he goes fast—he surges the

> whole way, and slows it down, he surges…you've got to run behind him (to know), he surges…" (Prokop, p. 110)

In *Sports Illustrated*, Reid also emphasized that I was diversifying my running skills:

> As John Walker and Rick Wohlhuter discovered last Saturday night in San Diego, a little learning is a dangerous thing. For Bayi has passed a cram course in indoor-mile strategy after just three meets, subtly revising his tactics while giving quality performances consistently. The indoor Bayi is a decidedly different runner from the impulsive African who set the track world on its ear outdoors: the astonishing front-runner who

The first of three times I appeared on the cover of *Track & Field News* during 1975.

> relished the idea of opening up 40 yards of daylight on the pack in the first half mile. Forced into a more conservative style by the tighter turns and shorter straights of the 160-yard indoor track, Bayi has mastered the concept of running with his rivals while distributing strength more evenly over the course of the race. And he probably has become a better runner as a result. (Reid, 1975)

I heard later that a supposed expert, when asked if there was any pace I couldn't win off of, said after I won in LA that Wohlhuter would beat me in San Diego because I don't "have great acceleration." Another coach, Joe Douglas, heard him and responded, "That's absurd! He accelerates but you don't notice. Bayi is the most efficient runner I've ever seen" (Prokop, p. 99).

//

I returned to New York for two more events. In my first time ever to face Eamonn Coghlan, the Irish star who would come to be called "The Chairman of the Boards" for his indoor racing skills, I ran a 3:41.2 to beat him in the Olympic Invitational 1500m. At the AAU Indoor Championships on February 28, I ran a 4:02.1 for my fifth victory on my US tour in five races. Then I headed for home, tired but satisfied with what I had accomplished over the past four weeks.

I told Sturak in the middle of my stay, "Now I learn, I think, 50 percent of the things that I want to learn. But I want to learn more" (Prokop, p. 111).

What was happening to me in the mid-1970s is hard to explain. Do you know when you are too busy with ideas, with business, with opportunities, yet you feel energized by it and want to grasp everything in your path? This can destroy some people. They overextend themselves and peter out in exhaustion. Or they reach for vices that ultimately destroy them. But when you are in this zone as an athlete or an artist or an entrepreneur, it's a special place where you can excel in ways you never knew.

I loved having a target on my back because I knew it would make me stronger. I wanted every challenger to give me his best. "I enjoy running,"

I told Reid of *Sports Illustrated* then. "And I enjoy even if anybody beat me. I don't mind it because it is racing. You can always lose because you are a human being."

When you are committed to learning, willing to risk defeat, and confident you can persevere to reach your goal, you are in a good place. In my early 20s, I was in that place.

And here's something that may surprise you: I actually look back and don't mind the media attention as much as I thought I did. I gave Sturak a hard time, but he was good to me. You can see how much I relied on him here in reconstructing my races during my first visit to the United States. He wanted to learn about me, and even if I don't think he got everything right about my background and personality, his intentions were true.

Western journalists were trying to make sense of the influx of African runners. How were we different from one another? What were the similarities? Yes, they were ignorant of my world as I was of theirs (though I eventually came to know who Mickey Mouse is). Africa was an unknown place to most Americans back then. Running put me in position to better understand the world, and for others to do so as well.

I had a few brief encounters with Sturak in later years, a quick hello and a laugh about when we first met—the annoying Time magazine reporter who interrupted us, the Beverly Hills Striders/Run for Fun T-shirt he gave me, the tedious questions about how I trained.

Sturak died in 2011 of Alzheimer's at the age of 79. I liked him. I also very much enjoy the way he described me in his essay: "I would add that Bayi is also the most *natural* runner I have ever seen. Most runners are distinguished by personal mannerisms and easily classified by style of stride (e.g., pusher/puller, driver/shuffler). But Bayi simply runs, like water flows or the wind blows" (Prokop, p. 99).

CHAPTER 10

The Secrets of My Success

RIFT VALLEYS ARE CREATED BY VIOLENT ACTIVITY UNDERNEATH THE earth's crust. Volcanoes, hot springs, geysers, deep lakes, and even earthquakes resulted as tectonic plates danced and collided with each other. As the highlands eroded and shaped into the Great Rift Valley that now cuts East Africa like a scythe, it filled with sediment that protected remains for the modern world to find and make sense of.

The Great Rift Valley was perfect for preserving all these sites and many others throughout East Africa—including the famous "Lucy" fossils in Ethiopia that date back 3.2 million years and the Laetoli Footprints that seem to indicate bipedalism preceded the increase in brain size in human evolution.

Based on discoveries like these, as well as significant finds in what is today South Africa, it's believed that all living humans descended from Africa. The Great Rift Valley specifically and Africa more generally are often called "the cradle of humankind."

The Great Rift Valley could also be called the cradle of distance-running excellence. In the major world marathons and Olympics today, the dominance of East Africans is almost a cliché. And most of those runners, especially from Kenya and Ethiopia, call the Rift Valley home, or at least their ancestors did. Much has been written over the past 50 years about why that is so. When Abebe Bikila, Mamo Wolde, Naftali Temu, Kip Keino, and others first started to gain international success in the 1960s and early 1970s, coaches, scientists, and Western journalists like Tom Sturak began to ask what the secret was.

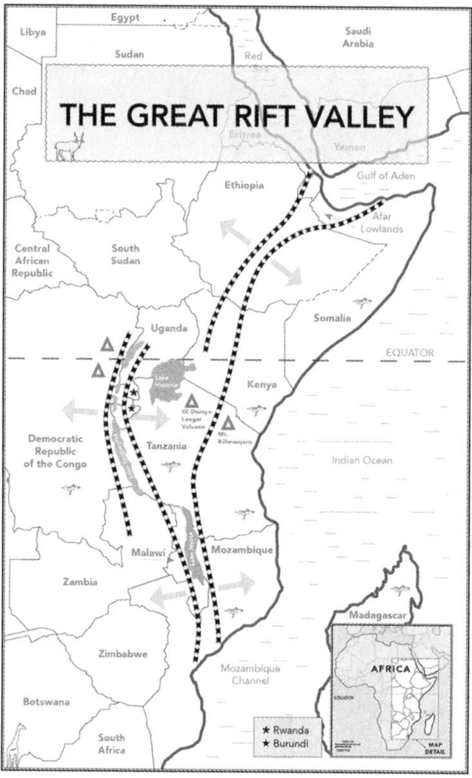

The Great Rift Valley, East Africa.

Altitude-training camps, nutritional analysis of the popular cornmeal known as ugali, and other hypotheses were still not the norm, but the quest to find the formula to east African running success was very much underway. The results were inconclusive; an odd assortment of conjecture, myth, stereotypes, and a little science in which it always seemed the inquirers were looking for the facts that fit their narrative.

The quest always seemed simplistic to me. I'm no evolutionary biologist or exercise physiologist or anthropologist, but understanding our success never seemed all that difficult. All of our ancestors had been hunting over long distances since the dawn of humanity.

Of course many great runners existed in East Africa long before the 1960s—I can think of excellent runners who were as good as me when I grew up in Arusha, but they didn't have the desire to continue. Only as sport became so globalized and marketable during my lifetime did anyone care. My timing was good. I became an adult at the right time to see the possibilities...but I'm a human being; I was always a runner.

Before African countries started gaining independence as the era of colonialism died in the 1960s, Scandinavians and New Zealanders were most often the successful long-distance runners, with an occasional American, Aussie, Brit, or other European thrown into the mix. When 19 Africans medaled in the distances at the 1968 and 1972 Olympics, the world took notice. Coaches sought out runners they could train. Sport administrators determined that fans were willing to pay to watch these elite athletes perform. Promising runners like me saw an opportunity to do something different than generations before us did. That's really not so hard to figure out. It's supply and demand. It's people experiencing unknown possibilities for a chance to seek their fame, fortune, or adventure.

It's economics and human aspirations, colliding like tectonic plates. Welcome to modern sport. Welcome to humanity.

Sure, there are factors to consider that make the Rift Valley seem ideal. Much of the region is at least 1,600 meters (a mile) high, with nearby mountains that give people a chance to produce additional red blood cells that help them function at altitude. As runners now know, if they and their coaches harness it effectively, altitude is advantageous when it comes to training for races. In these rural areas, even now but especially in the mid-20th century, transportation mostly consisted of walking and running, not wheels, to get from place to place. Whether it was a hut across the meadow or school or hunting or grazing fields 10 or 20 kilometers (roughly six to 12 miles) away, moving upright on two feet—and sometimes with speed—was the most convenient mode each day.

But I do find it interesting that people assume there's a magic key that unlocks the success of African runners over the past half century. Was there a common thread that explained why the Finns Paavo Nurmi and Ville

Ritola were champions? Or the Kiwis Peter Snell and Murray Halberg, or my contemporaries John Walker and Rod Dixon? What about the Brits who came after me, Sebastian Coe and Steve Ovett? These countrymen didn't all grow up the same way any more than Ethiopians Kenenisa Bekele and Haile Gebrselassie or Kenyans Kip Keino and Ben Jipcho…yet people look for a special ingredient that took East African runners to the top.

The most successful runners from the Great Rift Valley are not the norm; they are outliers by definition if they are the best in the world at what they do. Bell curves exist in sports as they do anywhere else in human endeavors. In fact, the beauty of sport is that we see the bell curve in fluid, beautiful motion more so than just about anywhere else you could name.

When you see Kenya's Eliud Kipchoge fly 26.2 miles in two hours, you're not witnessing a Rift Valley–raised runner doing what comes easily to everyone who grew up here. You're seeing a dedicated, talented, driven man with a lot of experienced professionals providing him support to achieve something amazing.

There are evolutionary advantages to growing up in different parts of the world for specific activities. There are also advantages to having access to experienced coaches, balanced nutrition, and a society that values your sport and wants to produce more successful athletes. We all have our own genes that we're born with and our own genetic responses to our environment that vary from person to person and can't be extrapolated to a whole society of people. God made each of us unique, and in that way life is not always fair…but that's a very different thing than saying a certain group of people is only successful because of how God made them.

David Epstein explored nature v. nurture in athletic performance in his groundbreaking 2013 book, *The Sports Gene.* He reports in great detail how athletes with particular traits excel in certain sports, but he also explains there is no perfect genetic makeup for an athlete. We are each very much individuals:

> In large part, humanity will continue to rely on chance and sports will continue to provide a splendid stage for the fantastic menagerie that is human biological diversity. Amid the pageantry of the Opening

> Ceremony at the 2016 Olympics in Rio de Janeiro, make sure to look at the extremes of the human physique. The 4'9" gymnast beside the 310-pound shot putter who is looking up at the 6'10" basketball player whose arms are seven and a half feet from fingertip to fingertip. Or the 6'4" swimmer who strides into the Olympic stadium beside his countryman, the 5'9" miler, both men wearing the same length pants.
>
> Our ethnic, geographic, and individual family histories have shaped the genetic information we carry at the nucleus of our every cell and, in turn, our bodies. It is breathtaking to think that, in the truest genetic sense, we are all a large family, and that the paths of our ancestors have left us so wonderfully distinct. In the very last line of his paradigm-shattering *On the Origin of Species*, Charles Darwin says this of his revelation that all the biological variation he sees springs from common ancestry: "...from so simple a beginning endless forms most beautiful and most wonderful have been, and are being, evolved."
>
> Because we are each unique, genetic science will continue to show that just as there is no one-size-fits-all medicine, there is no one-size-fits-all training program. If one sport or training method isn't working, it may not be the training. It may be you, in the very deepest sense. (Epstein, p. 289)

Thousands upon thousands of perfectly capable runners had dreams of being a world record holder or Olympic medalist but never did it. Those of us who have achieved it understand how difficult it is to reach that level, no matter how much talent or coaching or drive we have.

I return again and again to three principles in this book that ultimately determine our individual paths—sacrifice, commitment, and confidence. If you want three secrets, I say those are self-driven ones that you should embrace on your personal journey. They open more doors than any genetic predispositions and external conditions when it comes to finding success as a runner, scientist, teacher, or anything else...whether you grew up in a rift valley or at sea level...whether you have loving parents or never even knew them.

CHAPTER 11

"This Time, He Didn't Die"

I RETURNED FROM THE UNITED STATES IN MARCH 1975 TIRED BUT invigorated. I'd missed my girlfriend immensely. Sending Anna a few words on postcards from New York and Los Angeles wasn't enough space to say all I had on my mind. Talking to her for a few minutes from a phone booth before the long-distance charges got too outrageous just wasn't enough time to hear her voice.

All the time I was abroad, I kept my watch on Tanzanian time. It helped me to remember home, like a memory. I knew what my family was doing anytime I checked my watch. I didn't want to forget that, even when I was away. It helped me keep my mind together.

Soon after I was back home, when we finally did have the opportunity to talk at length again, she gave me some wonderful news. She was pregnant! In those days, an unmarried couple having a baby could be considered scandalous...a mistake. We did not see it that way. We even joked that the first child is for "training."

If I had left her and not taken on my responsibility, I'm sure there would have been gossip. But I had no intention of doing that. I was gainfully employed by the army and a world record–holding amateur runner. Our families supported us completely. There was no need to rush to get married, as far as we were concerned. I wasn't going anywhere. We trusted each other fully and knew we would get married someday.

Some men want to be chased by women when they travel. I had no temptation. I was concentrating on my racing and my training. I had my Anna; that was more than I could ask for.

Undefeated in the US, a baby on the way. The year was off to a great start…and it was just beginning.

//

Suleiman Nyambui and I joined the national team for training camp in Kibaha, about 30 kilometers (about 18.6 miles) outside Dar es Salaam. The army gave me leave, and the hostel we stayed at there made for an excellent training site. We had good food, and the dirt roads, though full of potholes, didn't have much traffic.

Nyambui and I had first met in 1971. He wasn't chosen for the Olympics, but the Tanzanian sporting establishment had their eyes on him. Nyambui joined Claver Kamanya and me midway through our 1973 European tour. We had run and roomed together before, but this was the first *extended* time to train together and he was showing how strong a competitor he could be. He was from the Lake Victoria region in far northwestern Tanzania, where local athletic officials first realized his potential as a runner. He had raced in international meets, including the record-breaking Christchurch field. But he was still working as a teacher, and the world didn't yet know how good an athlete he was.

In Kibaha, still without a proper distance coach, we pushed each other, man. I had spent so much time doing sprint training so I could get used to running hard while in oxygen debt. Then, my winter was spent racing in the tight spaces of American arenas. With Nyambui, I relished a chance to run unleashed again. I wanted to improve my endurance. Nyambui, an emerging 5000m and 10,000m guy, gave me that opportunity. We were a formidable pair in workouts. Tempo runs were intense. He forced me to go longer, building my stamina, while I forced him to go faster, building his speed.

We were brothers working together for Team Tanzania—ready to inspire and open the doors to talented runners from all over the country!

On the track, I certainly felt like I had proven to myself that mentally and physically, I could respond to anything the competition wanted to throw at me. But that's not the same as believing I was unstoppable. I knew how good Walker, Coghlan, Wohlhuter, Dixon, Liquori, and others were, and I also knew they weren't stupid. It was clear they were training so they could keep me close enough early in races and still have enough speed and stamina to pick me off at the end.

People were asking me how fast I could go, but I'm not God: "If you can tell me the day on which you are going to die," I said back then, "I will tell you when I will run 3:30 for 1500 meters or 3:47 for a mile" (Prokop, p. 112).

I wasn't focused on records; I needed to determine how I could continue to win races with a whole bunch of guys nipping at my heels. Soon after returning from my American introduction to indoor racing, I did something completely different: I left the track to compete at the Cinque Mulini in San Vittore Olona, Italy. Cinque Mulini is one of the most storied cross country races in the world and also one of the most beautiful. The course goes past five water mills (the "cinque mulini") along the Olona River in northern Italy. I ran the 9.5K (approximately...they didn't measure the old course exactly) race in 30:18.4 for the victory, ahead of New Zealanders Euan Robertson and my old friend John Walker.

I soon had a good reason to expand my training routine with Nyambui. I got an invitation to an event that May in Kingston, Jamaica. The name of the race said it all: the Dream Mile.

It was the centerpiece of an event known as the Martin Luther King Jr. International Freedom Games, which was an outstanding track meet sponsored by the Southern Christian Leadership Conference that King and other American civil rights leaders had founded. It was held in King's memory after his assassination, from 1969 into the mid-'80s. Most years it was held in the United States, but in 1975 we were going to Jamaica.

In early May, I returned to Italy, this time in the southern part of the country. I set a national record in winning a 1000m on the track in Formia, then captured an 800m victory in nearby Caserta two days later.

My interval workouts were often alone. I did 400- and 600-meter reps when I was getting ready for the 800m. Though my Italian races were shorter, all spring I was already locked into longer sets, like 1200 meters. I needed speed and endurance to prepare for longer events like the 1500m and the mile. With a solid base from running with Nyambui and a wide range of distances on and off the track that spring, I felt I was prepared for whoever would be in the field. I returned home briefly to see Anna. In exactly one week, I needed to be ready for my highly anticipated return to the Western Hemisphere.

//

The Dream Mile was a great name for the race, and not just as a way to remember King's "I Have a Dream" speech. The field of runners that race organizer Bert Lancaster assembled for his meet was outstanding, as usual. There was Marty Liquori, who had run a 3:53.6 mile two years earlier at the King Games. Also, Eamonn Coghlan of Ireland, who was the current young star at Liquori's alma mater, Villanova University; Rick Wohlhuter, the 880-yard world record holder; and Tony Waldrop, the indoor mile world record holder at 3:55 who had run nine consecutive sub-four-minute miles in 1974 with a PR of 3:53.2.

Reggie McAfee, the first African-American to run a sub-four mile (3:59.3), Great Britain's Walter Wilkinson, and Jamaica's Sylvan Barrett completed the lineup. Pretty much every top miler in the world was there except for Ben Jipcho, who was now a professional, and John Walker.

But often, such as at the Olympics, that much talent can hinder the possibility of a record-setting day. Expectations are too high. Runners are cautious and tactical at the expense of speed, regardless of what they may state publicly in the buildup to the race. We all were required to attend a press conference a day before the race. A big Dream Mile trophy was unveiled. "Who is going to take this trophy?" someone asked. The discussion was mostly about winning the race, not about setting a new world record time, which at that point Jim Ryun had held for almost exactly eight years.

Besides, I had just reached Kingston two days before the race after 23 hours of flying with four layovers. Because I was so stiff after my travels, I did a fairly strenuous workout the day after I arrived. I ran a few warm-up laps, then three 600s at a brisk pace, jogged another 5,000 meters, and then reeled off a 4:10 mile. That may have seemed too much of a workload just before a big race, but I knew what my body needed. I wanted to win that trophy and believed I could do it. Still, I did not have dreams of setting a world record.

I did find time to shop for record albums. That was my way to relax. In the United States, I bought pop and country—Jackson Five, the Commodores, Diana Ross, Kenny Rogers, Dolly Parton, Don Williams. In Jamaica, I had the chance to get reggae and Caribbean music such as Bob Marley and Boney M before I even left the airport.

Not surprisingly, the big question put to me and the other runners was whether I would push the pace. There were doubts that I would do so before my 1500m world record in Christchurch the year before, even though I stated pretty clearly that I would run from the front. This time, however, after my successful first season of indoor racing and my experimentation the previous summer, it was a legitimate question. The other runners' comments even made it seem that they wanted me to act as their pacer in order to help them establish personal-best times.

"I'd prefer to see Bayi take it out," Coghlan told *Sports Illustrated*. "So far this season, in any race I've run, I've been out there myself in the lead and I haven't been pulled right from the start. So I'd like him to take it out to get the best out of me."

On the other hand, the two Americans, Liquori and Wohlhuter, stated publicly that they expected me to hold back.

I was coy: "I know what pace I will run, but it is my secret," I said.

//

The atmosphere was electric at the National Stadium, like a carnival. Jamaicans love their sprinters, but the eyes of all 36,000 fans were focused on the Dream Mile. Each of us got a detailed description of ourselves at the starting line as we were introduced to the packed stadium. I got the biggest roar of all—bigger even than Jamaica's own runner, Sylvan Barrett—when the announcer shouted, "This mahn runs his races like a mahn who has stolen the mangoes and is running from the police!" (Liquori and Myslenski, p. 186).

He described exactly what I was about to do.

I started on the inside and immediately ran to the front. Within 75 meters, I was a thief on my own on that sultry 70-degree night, creating space between me and the cops. After one lap, a relatively slow 56.9 seconds, I had 12 yards on the field.

I was gliding for the next 300 meters and opened up a nearly 20-yard gap. But as I neared the halfway point, I turned back for a quick look. Coghlan clearly realized they had let me escape and he needed to close the gap. Liquori went too, letting Coghlan pull him along. Both were known as kickers and surely felt they still had a chance. They were gaining as I passed the half-mile point in 1:56.6, still 10 yards in front.

Coghlan closed quickly on the backstretch of the third lap. I could hear his footsteps just behind me. I looked tired, even a little hunched around the curve, but I was holding back after my surge from the start line. Coghlan was churning and looking strong, but I knew he used up a lot of energy to try and reel me in. With Liquori nipping at his heels and barking at him to pass me, Coghlan was aiming for me as we neared the straightaway to complete the third lap. He was pushing so hard it almost looked like he thought *this* was the final lap.

I was too far out in lane 1, and Coghlan slipped past my left shoulder on the inside. He almost had half a step on me until I immediately sprinted ahead of him. Liquori was four steps behind, but I'm sure he was thinking he had me in his grasp as well.

I had to bury them before they could form the belief that they'd broken me.

As the gun sounded for the final lap, our splits were as follows: me, 2:55.3; Coghlan, 2:55.7; Liquori, 2:56.2. I kept a smooth stride and accelerated, opening up a slight gap on the curve. When Liquori moved beside Coghlan to pass him, they inadvertently bumped elbows as Coghlan tried to hold off his fellow Villanovan. Both were only a few steps behind me with 275 yards to go. That led to Coghlan attempting another surge that carried him to within a step of me. I again withstood the challenge. In the final 220 yards, Liquori and Coghlan fought each other for position while I was lengthening my stride, all alone. Liquori broke loose of Coghlan at the crown of the final bend, but by then I was free and clear. I widened the gap and crossed the finish with a 10-meter lead, thanks to a 55.7-second final quarter.

I slowed down but kept moving around the curve, still by myself. The crowd was buzzing—still as loud as they were when Coghlan took his brief lead on the third lap. I acknowledged the fans with a couple of half-hearted

With no words, only numbers, the July 1975 *Track & Field News* cover said it all.

hand raises, thrilled at how I'd held off two determined runners but too tired to do more! Finally, the public-address announcer gave the news: I had run a 3:51.0. I stopped, gave a quick bunny hop, touched my hands to my toes, thrust my hands in the air, and continued my victory lap. The entire Chevron-440 synthetic track felt like it was my domain.

Jim Ryun had held the mile world record since July 17, 1966. He had run 3:51.3 that day in Berkeley, California. Then on June 23, 1967, in Bakersfield, California, he lowered that mark to 3:51.1—a race in which a 17-year-old Liquori became just the third American high school athlete to ever run a mile under four minutes. No one else had ever run under 3:52. I had bettered it by the narrowest of margins—the first African to hold the mile record, just as I was the first African to break the 1500m world mark. Now I was also a member of another exclusive club—men who had held both records at the same time. Other than Ryun and me, only six others had done that at that time (see Appendix B for a full list).

None of that was going through my head at the time, though. I felt some relief, to be honest. Despite heavy travel, the possibility of fatigue, and tactics that were designed to take me down, I had overcome the best field of milers ever assembled. As one announcer declared at the conclusion of the race, "This time he didn't die."

If Coghlan and Liquori had collaborated better, they might have had a shot. But I surprised them by pressing the matter more than they expected right from the gun, and retained the lead when challenged. That is what a champion does—acts as the aggressor even when being chased.

Liquori said the two of them never talked about strategy before the race. "That was the most tired I ever was at the end of a race," he said, looking back nearly 50 years later. "I didn't want to run any extra yards and I expended so much energy getting around Eamonn that by the time I got to the straightaway, Bayi took the legs out of me."

When asked recently, Coghlan said that my Christchurch run "frightened me so much that my dreams of being a great runner were almost shattered, believing I'd never match his unprecedented opening-lap splits if I ever got a chance to race against him." Given the chance in Kingston,

Coghlan boldly challenged me. "I couldn't believe I was on Filbert's shoulder attempting to pass my new running 'god,'" Coghlan said. "Running faster than ever in my life, my legs began to quiver and buckle beneath."

I was focused and determined. I wore them down. "Filbert was caught by Eamonn Coghlan and Marty Liquori with one lap to go but he surged away again in an unbelievable demonstration of power and determination," wrote blogger Haile Tuluwami. "Despite his strenuous front running all over the race, he ended up looking much fresher than all his rivals" (Tuluwami, 2011).

Liquori's explanation in *Sports Illustrated* vindicated every choice I made in the race and my training in preparation for the Dream Mile. I didn't leave it to chance to be navigating for space beside another runner. And I didn't give them enough time to capitalize on the momentum they gained in the final 600 meters:

> "I think Coghlan and I both made a mistake on the third lap," Liquori said. "Bayi had slowed up noticeably and I yelled at Eamonn to pass him. I think if we had both passed him then, psychologically it would have been good. I think we could have worked it so that it would have been very tough for him to get by us. In that last lap, I had some tactical problems. I thought both Coghlan and I were going to beat Bayi, but what happened was, we both began trying to pass him at the same time going around the second-to-last turn. I had to get out in the second lane, and when I tried to go by, Eamonn bumped me with an elbow." (Reid, 1975)

As running journalists analyzed the race later, they pointed out that although my splits were pretty consistent—56.9, 59.7, 58.7, and 55.7—I did it in fits and starts. I sped up and slowed down numerous times to build my lead, conserve energy, and then put down several challenges. Like a car in Dar traffic, that is not an efficient use of the machine. They also noted that I ran on the outer edge of the first lane during part of the race. This meant I probably covered several additional yards over four laps, which was completely unnecessary since I was in the lead. It's also what gave Coghlan an opening to try to shoot by me late in the third lap. I have no idea why I did that. Sometimes when you're in a groove—even if you're well prepared—the little things slip by.

"Had he run close to the kerb and at a more consistent pace, he would surely have been under 3:50," wrote John Cobley in *Racing Past*. "He seemed in control the whole race and was able to take the kick out of his two main rivals with classic catch-me-if-you-can front-runner tactics. And he still had to run a world-record time to win the race" (Cobley, 2013).

Sports Illustrated, May 26, 1975.

Ron Reid of *Sports Illustrated* accurately recapped my crazy week:

> Bayi led wire to wire, opening a gaping lead early, then losing nearly all of it, then opening up again to win by 10 yards. He did it despite a 23-hour plane trip from Africa to Jamaica via Rome, London, Montreal and New York, which landed him in Kingston 48 hours before the race. And he did it despite a heavy workout the day before the meet. Halfway through the race Bayi twisted around in a sort of golfer's follow-through for a look back at his opposition, possibly to see what other traditional rules of running he could violate.
>
> For a middle-distance runner of merely superb ability, any of these factors might have been enough to deny victory, let alone a world record. But the 21-year-old Bayi is extraordinary and he turned the Dream Mile, as it was billed, into vivid reality for a crowd of 36,000 in sultry National Stadium. (Reid, 1975)

Liquori said years later that fans underestimated how smart my training and race tactics were. It's easy to not appreciate how to succeed with that approach because you don't see the frontrunner conserving his energy. "For 100 years, you jogged three laps and then sprinted like a stock car race for a lap," Liquori said. "Filbert changed the race. It's a drag race, and we're just going to go fast until the engine blows up."

//

As in Christchurch, my pacing had lifted virtually everyone to their best efforts. Six of eight runners went sub-four minutes. Liquori logged the fastest runner-up mile performance ever in 3:52.2, the fifth-fastest time ever at the distance. "It's scary though," Liquori said. "I really don't know if Bayi was even *ready* for this race" (Liquori and Myslenski, p. 187).

Coghlan, just 22 years old (eight months older than me), had his first major international success. He set an Irish and European record with his 3:53.3 showing, the 11th fastest mile ever and almost seven seconds better than his PR from just two weeks earlier. "For three quarters I felt great, really within myself," Coghlan said later. "The last lap, though, took quite a bit out of me. As soon as I caught Bayi the second time he took off again, and when Marty passed me, I lost my confidence a bit.... But it was a great race and I'm really delighted I was part of it" (Liquori and Myslenski, p. 187).

Wohlhuter, an 800m specialist who was fourth with a PR of 3:53.8, perhaps best summed up the ambivalence my opponents were feeling:

Capping a big month on May 31, 1975, I won the Emsley Carr Mile at the British International Games at the Crystal Palace National Sports Centre in London, with a time of 3 minutes, 55 seconds.

"The mile will be the death of me," he said. "I keep running better times and getting lower places" (Reid, 1975).

As long as I was the one at the top, I was spared that frustration.

What I did feel was gratitude. At having the health and the opportunity through my army service to be able to run at this high level when we as amateurs didn't get paid. I was grateful at being challenged, and I knew my competitors were grateful to me for helping them to be better. This, my friends, is what competition does to us all. Whether you're the predator or the prey, you discover something about yourself.

Even though Coghlan said after the Dream Mile, "I wonder what would happen if he was really pushed," trust me when I say that without him and Liquori trying to chase me down, I don't set the mile world record. Without Walker's push over the final 50 meters in Christchurch the year before, I don't set the 1500m world record. I'll never forget them for that. If no one is pushing you, you relax. You can't measure your limits if no one is pushing you. Your competitors help you find your capacity.

Liquori was gracious to me. He said he was never frustrated at losing that race because his legs were dead and I deserved the win. He later told me that he usually drank a lot of Coke, but heading into that race with me he'd gotten it into his head that I was from Africa and must eat some all-natural, pure diet. He chose to give up sugar for weeks ahead of the race. When he saw me put huge teaspoons of sugar into my tea at a banquet after that world record, he was annoyed he had wasted all those chances to drink a soda.

//

I wasn't done with big moments on the track in 1975. Two weeks after Kingston, my 3:55.5 at London's Crystal Palace meant that I took the prestigious Emsley Carr Mile and added my name to the red leather-bound book that all its winners sign. Roger Bannister himself presented me the trophy. Two seconds back in third place was Polish steeplechaser Bronisław Malinowski, whom I later found out had been training with the New Zealanders. Rod Dixon said Malinowski was influenced by me; he was running miles and 1500s to improve his speed. In sixth place was a young Steve Ovett, the first time we ever raced each other.

A month after that, on June 27–28, I won the 800m and the 5000m on successive days in Lourenço Marques, Mozambique. Those dates are significant. It was a track meet to celebrate the end of a decade of war with Portugal. Independence had just been declared on June 25, and I wanted to show my support to our neighbors.

Walker soon lowered the world record further. I was not in Gothenburg, Sweden, when he became the first man to break 3:50, clocking a 3:49.4 on August 12. Still, my place in history was secure as the first African to hold the world record—it made me part of the line of progression for the inevitable lowering of times in track and field's most storied event.

I wanted an Olympic gold medal, and Walker's ascension heightened interest for our rematch in 1976. Unfortunately, the next chapter in our rivalry involved something neither of us had control over.

I didn't die in Christchurch or Kingston. But in Montreal, I never got a chance to live.

1975 MLK JR. INTERNATIONAL GAMES
National Stadium, Kingston, Jamaica
May 17, 1975

The Dream Mile

1.	Filbert Bayi	TANZANIA	3:51.0	WR
2.	Marty Liquori	UNITED STATES	3:52.2	PR
3.	Eamonn Coghlan	IRELAND	3:53.3	NR
4.	Rick Wohlhuter	UNITED STATES	3:53.7	PR
5.	Tony Waldrop	UNITED STATES	3:57.7	
6.	Reggie McAfee	UNITED STATES	3:59.5	
7.	Walter Wilkinson	GREAT BRITAIN	4:06.2	
8.	Sylvan Barrett	JAMAICA		

CHAPTER 12

Mataifa yetu yalitusihi tujali wenzetu

EVEN MORE THAN GRATEFUL, IN 1975 I FELT BLESSED. ANNA AND I welcomed our firstborn into the world, a son we named Engelbert.

Every parent is surely in awe of their own newborn child. I'm no different in that way. However, I couldn't help but think about how my own father never got this humbling experience. He never got to hold me, or smile with my mother as they watched me sleep. Like me, he traveled for business a lot while his wife was pregnant. While I could choose relatively quick trips to East Africa, Europe—even Peking, China—he died alone, away from his wife, 50 miles from home.

Anna took to mothering as gracefully as my own mother had done, which was no surprise to me. She took care of all the details...feeding, rocking him to sleep, keeping him healthy. I did my best to keep up with her, but thank God she was always the one in charge of our family. And I just kept thanking God that I was there for Anna and Engelbert.

I was there.

//

So much had changed for me personally since my last Olympic appearance in 1972. I went to Munich an unknown 19-year-old, an army private who barely knew how to train and race, and struggled mightily to communicate in English. With the Montreal Games looming in July 1976,

I was a two-time world record holder whom track and field fans wanted to see in a showdown with my greatest rival. I had been asked a million questions about my revolutionary racing style, my unorthodox training methods, my childhood, my country, and my competitors. I had been on the cover of *Track & Field News* four times and even *Sports Illustrated.*

There was much anticipation about a Walker-Bayi duel in the offseason prior to the 1976 Olympics, as the November 1975 *Track & Field News* cover shows.

I was a father and a lieutenant in the army, and I had traveled around the world. I was far removed from the days of chasing my dog, Simba, in the bush around Karatu. Above all, I was a grown man.

The excitement I felt at the prospect of winning an Olympic medal—which would be Tanzania's first—had been building for at least a year.

When Walker broke my mile mark in August 1975, Montreal became the next major international stage where the current 1500m world record holder (me) and current mile world record holder (him) could face off. Though I'd beaten him four times in 1975 and he'd beaten me twice, he was now considered the man on top. He even had a better 1500m time than me that year. I certainly was not overconfident. Walker's 3:49.4 mile was all the proof I needed that I would have my work cut out for me at the 1500m in Montreal.

I have always said that an athlete must first and foremost be his or her own coach. Since I couldn't move up the Olympics on the calendar, my coach was preaching patience as 1976 arrived.

I did my best to rein in my enthusiasm so as not to waste my energy or let myself stray from my schedule. There were reports that malaria was harming my ability to train, but that was really not true. Any effects I felt were minor compared to other outbreaks I've experienced in my life. By then, I had plenty of experience racing. I simply didn't want to overdo my travel and competition in an Olympic year.

I returned to the US for the indoor circuit, but one of the only outdoor meets I ran in 1976 was the opening of Tanzania's first Tartan track, in Zanzibar. When I ran a 3:34.8 in the 1500m on that fast surface, I felt sure I had a shot at the gold medal. I was still in charge of my own training and focused on building speed and stamina, which I was doing quite well. I was as confident as I had ever been in my planning and execution.

Such is the randomness of the Olympics (and life) that the best-laid plans can unravel with little notice.

//

Since 1964, South Africa had been banned from competing in the Olympic Games because of its apartheid policy and white minority-ruled government. In 1970, South Africa was officially expelled from the International Olympic Committee as well. Even outside the Olympic Movement, the international sporting world generally held to an informal embargo of the racist regime.

Sports was definitely entwined with politics then, as now. During this early postcolonial period, Black Africa didn't have much sway at the United Nations and in other economic and political entities. But sports federations were a different matter. Some newly independent countries even applied for IOC membership before applying for UN membership.

In my return to the US indoor season early in 1976, I fought to hold off Rod Dixon (left) and Paul Cummings at the Jack in Box Indoor Games in San Diego. Dixon slipped by me for a narrow victory of seven-tenths of a second.

In 1966, many African countries created the Supreme Council of Sport in Africa, which had the expressed purpose of fighting against colonialism and apartheid on the continent. Specifically, the SCSA pushed for the exclusion of South Africa and white-ruled Rhodesia from international sports competitions. Black Africa showed its power in 1968. The IOC was planning to bring South Africa back into the Olympics, but when African countries threatened to boycott the Mexico City Games, the

IOC backed down. A similar threat was made prior to the 1972 Olympics, and the IOC still kept South Africa out.

When New Zealand's famed national rugby team, the All Blacks, planned a three-month tour of South Africa for summer 1976, there was widespread condemnation in Africa and other parts of the world. The SCSA had spent months early in the year saying it would push the IOC to punish New Zealand if the tour went ahead as planned. Then, on June 16, less than a week before the tour was to begin, South Africa's government massacred several hundred anti-apartheid protestors, many of them schoolchildren.

The protests came in Soweto, a black township outside of Johannesburg created when South Africa's government segregated blacks from whites, decades earlier. Students and teachers were responding to a recent law that Afrikaans, the language of the oppressive government, be the language of instruction in schools. Students went on strike in April, and the protests intensified until they came to a head with the deadly police response.

With pressure rising on New Zealand, the South African tour was delayed. Tanzanian President Julius Nyerere rallied African nations to prepare a boycott of the 1976 Montreal Games, which were set to begin July 17. The demands of the Organization of African Unity (OAU) were clear. It insisted that the IOC ban New Zealand from competing because the national rugby team had legitimized the South African government by planning to be guests there.

A spokesperson for the New Zealand Olympic Committee called the demands "illogical," as the tour had been arranged by the New Zealand Rugby Union, an autonomous body that had nothing to do with the Olympics. He also pointed out that 26 other countries had played sport in South Africa during the past year.

That may have been true, but it didn't take into account the immediate tragedy in Soweto. It also didn't recognize the important statement it would make to not allow rugby—a pastime transported worldwide through colonialism and the most popular sport in both countries—to be played. Stopping this lucrative tour would have an economic and symbolic impact on South Africa and be more likely to capture the attention of the world.

The OAU met in early July in Port Louis, Mauritius, and told the IOC to choose between New Zealand and the OAU. There was still a lot of uncertainty as to who would do what: could so many different African nations and cultures band together on this major decision? Would New Zealand's far-right prime minister call off the tour? And whose side would the IOC take?

One week before the Games were to begin, my country became the first to announce it would boycott. The question was whether the rest of the continent would follow Tanzania's lead. Several countries did. The IOC announced the day before the Olympics were to start that since rugby was not an Olympic sport, they had no grounds to remove New Zealand from the Games.

The next day, when New Zealand announced the All Blacks had left for South Africa, much of Africa stepped into the boycott. Even as athletes entered the Olympic Stadium, it wasn't clear which countries were in and out. Preliminary events had already taken place in some sports.

In all, 26 countries boycotted the Opening Ceremonies, and three more joined after taking part in them. About 20 of those nations had already arrived in Canada before their national leaders called them home. Athletes waited for buses in the Olympic Village to take them back to the airport. Kenya's foreign minister, James Osogo, put out a statement just hours before the Opening Ceremonies: "The government and the people of Kenya hold the view that principles are more precious than medals." The decision by the IOC not to ban New Zealand, Osogo said, would give "comfort and respectability to the South African racist regime and encourage it to continue to defy world opinion."

I never got on a plane. I was working at the air wing in Dar when the announcement of the Tanzanian boycott came. I was not surprised, but I would be lying if I said it didn't pain me to know I would not get my chance to win an Olympic medal. Unlike the pain of my brothers and sisters in Soweto, though, mine quickly subsided. They were killed for demonstrating for their rights in a country that gave them none. They were not soldiers.

More than 300 athletes were affected, and some events had to be cancelled or rescheduled. My absence was discussed more than just about anybody's as the fallout became clear. "Athletics events will be particularly affected by the absence of Filbert Bayi from Tanzania, who holds the world record in the 1500m and John Akii-Bua of Uganda, world record-holder in the 400 metres hurdles," reported the BBC.

///

In most analyses about the boycott that dealt with the effect on competition, track and field was considered the biggest casualty. The explosion of African talent that had asserted itself over the past decade and a half in the middle and long distances was nowhere to be seen in Montreal. The top performers' nationalities looked very much as they did before the 1960s—northern Europeans, New Zealanders, and the occasional Brit and American. Finland's Lasse Viren repeated his sweep of the 5000m and 10,000m from 1972.

With a few notable exceptions, every medal from 800 meters to the marathon went to a European. Alberto Juantorena of Cuba completed a rare double with a win in the 400m and a world record of 1:43.5 in the 800m. American Rick Wohlhuter placed third in the 800m, while his countryman Frank Shorter, the gold medalist in Munich, took silver in the marathon. Dick Quax of New Zealand took silver in the 5000m.

It was Quax's teammate who was the most notable non-European of all. Without me there, John Walker became the clear favorite in the 1500m. Supporters of the boycott noted with some bitterness that Quax and Walker benefitted greatly from their African opponents not being in Montreal. But they never said they agreed with their country's or the IOC's stance. Walker had personally turned down invitations to race in

South Africa. They and Dixon and other prominent New Zealand athletes joined their country's anti-apartheid activists in appealing to their government to disallow the tour. They were unsuccessful. Ultimately, they were athletes who wanted to compete, and given the chance they did just that. It just so happened that their nation and my continent were at the center of a major disagreement.

Walker narrowly beat out Ivo Van Damme of Belgium and Paul-Heinz Wellman of West Germany for gold in the 1500m. His victorious time of 3:39.17 was really slow compared to the marks he and I had been putting up over the past three years. The question of who would have won between the two of us will remain forever unanswered.

There weren't television sets on the Tanzanian mainland in 1976, but I did follow the Olympics and Walker's win in the newspapers. It's not uncommon for championship races to go slow, but when I saw his mark, I felt that had been my race to win. I never did talk with him during or after the Games about it. In interviews, he said he was disappointed he couldn't face me. I believe that is true. You want to beat everybody to be a champion. But you can only beat those you line up against.

Walker and I have never talked much about politics, but we always had a mutual respect for each other. Asked in 2021 about his gold medal, Walker said this: "Filbert and I never discussed the '76 boycott as I remember. I was really sad and disappointed about it because I was in great shape and I wanted Filbert in the race. I had imagined our last lap together, with us both running flat out and smashing the world record. With Filbert not being there at the Olympics, it took the gloss off the 1500m for me."

I've been asked many times through the years if I agreed that the boycott was the right decision. I've never wavered. Sure, I was disappointed that I wouldn't get to run; who wouldn't be? I had been training four years for that moment. I was ready. But at the end of the day, the effect on me was that I didn't have a chance to win a medal. If that's my biggest problem, I've lived a blessed life.

The far more important issue was showing our unity with our African brothers and sisters who were dealing with injustice so positive change could be made. In Swahili, we say, *Mataifa yetu yalitusihi tujali wenzetu*: "Our nations humbly require us to respect our friends and partners." It should be relevant every day of our lives, but in some moments, some decisions, we must act on it and not shy away from our responsibility. The circumstances swirling around the sports world and South Africa in summer 1976 required decisive action.

Many American athletes—even decades later—were furious with US President Jimmy Carter's boycott of the Moscow Olympics four years later after the Soviet Union's invasion of Afghanistan. President Carter was responding to aggression, just as the OAU did, but it was a very different situation. The American boycott was over a military action the sports community couldn't control. The anti-apartheid boycott stemmed from sport being complicit in a government's abuse and violence.

The African boycott meant that my Tanzanian brother Suleiman Nyambui (right) and I missed the 1976 Olympics.

I felt that President Nyerere did a brave thing in leading the way when he had the opportunity. I was proud to be a Tanzanian when he asked us to make that sacrifice.

The 1976 African-led protest was the first mass Olympic boycott. It isn't remembered as well as President Carter's action to lead a 65-nation boycott of the Moscow Olympics, nor the USSR's retaliatory 1984 boycott of the Los Angeles Games. The immediate analysis of the Montreal boycott was that African countries made a disastrous tactical error. But looking back, that doesn't hold up.

In the short term, the boycott boosted the morale of the young protesters in Soweto at an agonizing time for them. They saw that their brothers and sisters from around the continent were willing to make a small sacrifice in a show of solidarity with them. The boycott raised the consciousness of people around the globe who at that point largely were not paying attention to the institutionalized racism in South Africa. The world saw unified action from a continent that, if they ever thought about it at all, they mischaracterized as being a place only decimated by war, colonialism, corruption, and factional fighting.

In his autobiography, Bruce Kidd, a former Canadian Olympic runner who was an anti-apartheid and athletes' rights activist at the time of the Montreal Games, pointed out that international federations in soccer, swimming, and track and field expelled South Africa as members within days of the Montreal boycott.

"Shortly after Montreal, the IOC stepped up its active support for the anti-apartheid campaign and Africa stayed. In 1978, under new political leadership, China joined the IOC. These decisions prevented a worldwide split in Olympic sports. In Africa's case, I've always felt that one of the reasons was the opportunity the anti-apartheid campaign gave it to refashion the Olympics as genuinely non-racial. It was the 'boycott that worked'" (Kidd, p. 250).

As an example of changing attitudes, when the South Africa rugby team toured New Zealand in 1981, protests and civil disobedience followed them everywhere they went. Anti-apartheid activists occupied one stadium, which resulted in the cancellation of a match. Soon afterward, New Zealand joined the informal boycott of South Africa that most other countries had long recognized. Desmond Tutu, who was bishop of Lesotho at the time of the 1976 riots and won the 1984 Nobel Peace Prize for his dedication and action to dismantling apartheid, said the global sporting effort to ignore South Africa was "the sanction that hurt the supporters of apartheid the most."

When asked in those years by reporters or when invited to presentations, I spoke out against the South African government. Sam Ramsamy, chair of the South Africa Non-Racial Olympic Committee (SAN-ROC), called my lost 1976 Olympics "a withdrawal that was a sacrifice in support of the oppressed people in South Africa." He often would praise me in meetings dealing with sport and social issues. Ramsamy and other anti-apartheid leaders were tireless in their devotion to the cause. For them to acknowledge me like that meant a great deal.

In June 1983, Ramsamy chaired the International Conference on Sanctions Against Apartheid Sport in London. The meeting, held by the Association of National Olympic Committees (ANOC), gave me the opportunity to share my experience and how sport was an important part of the struggle to change the racist government policy.

The apartheid government didn't officially end until 1994, and South Africa didn't return to the Olympic Movement until 1992, after a long and gradual series of reforms in the country. But, "The Montreal Games really changed the world," Courtney W. Mason, a researcher who studied the 1976 Olympics, said on the 40th anniversary of the boycott. "Historians will say it's really the economic sanctions that ended apartheid and that's true. But what was really important about Montreal was that the word 'apartheid' appeared on the front page of every newspaper in the world, and people started talking about the issue and pressuring their own governments" (Riga, 2016).

June 16 is now a public holiday in South Africa. Appropriately enough, it is known as Youth Day.

//

When life seems unfair or unjust, whether for individuals or groups of people, change can seem impossibly slow if it feels like it's happening at all. Revolutions don't happen overnight. But if you want to see an example of how the world can change in a relatively short period of time, look at what happened with rugby in South Africa in 1995.

The rugby-proud country was awarded the World Cup—the first major sporting event to take place in South Africa after the end of apartheid. South Africa, despite its love of the sport, had never been allowed to compete in a rugby World Cup before. In the final held in Johannesburg, 30 minutes away from Soweto, South Africa defeated New Zealand in extra time.

Nelson Mandela, political prisoner for 27 years, Nobel Peace Prize laureate, and the first black president of South Africa, presented the Webb Ellis Cup to François Pienaar, the captain of the Springboks—the name for the national team that was one of the country's most powerful symbols of oppression for decades. Mandela himself wore a Springboks shirt and cap.

The story of that World Cup and Mandela's embrace of the team as a means to unite the fragile new government was later told on the big screen in "Invictus," with Morgan Freeman playing Mandela and Matt Damon playing Pienaar.

Mandela himself delivered a quote at the inaugural Laureus World Sports Awards in 2000 that has been repeated thousands of times since. "Sport has the power to change the world," he said. "It has the power to inspire. It has the power to unite people in a way that little else does. It speaks to youth in a language they understand."

People often say that sport and politics shouldn't mix, yet sport and politics are part of every society. They will clash at times. The question isn't whether they should mix, but rather what side you choose when they do. You must be confident, committed, and willing to sacrifice when your moment arrives to support a just cause. Tanzania and much of Black Africa rose to the occasion when asked to do so. I'm proud to have been part of that.

CHAPTER 13

Transitions

AFTER THE 1976 OLYMPIC FLAME WAS EXTINGUISHED, THE WORLD got back to other matters. I had important business to take care of in Same District in Kilimanjaro Region: it was time to ask Anna's parents for permission to marry their daughter.

Anna and I leaving St. Joseph Cathedral after saying our vows on October 10, 1977. One of the men whom we passed under was Davis Mwamunyange, who later was in charge of The Tanzania People's Defence force. He is the sword captain on the highest step, third from the right in the photo.

I wasn't worried about their response. They knew I was a devoted partner and father. Plus, I reasoned, you can't reject a champion! I still felt the pressure, though, as I traveled to their home. This was an official visit, in which I was to bring a delegation of friends, offer a bull goat or a cow or a sheep as a promise, and plan a wedding date.

We chose October 10 of the following year. It was a small military ceremony. I was promoted to captain in 1977, but my army salary didn't allow for extravagances. We were married at the St. Joseph Cathedral in Dar es Salaam. As we left the church, Anna and I passed underneath sabers held by soldiers for an escorted motorcade to the reception at the Oysterbay Police Mess.

Anna and I relax at the reception on our big day.

Army tradition dictates that when the groom arrives, the "sword captains" pour bottles of beer over him. As it turned out, one of my sword captains, Davis Mwamunyange, later became General Mwamunyange and Chief of the Tanzania People's Defence Force, in charge of the country's military from 2007–2017.

Once the army uniform is drenched with beer, you go shower, change clothes, and return. Meanwhile, the bride, dry and smiling, entertains the guests. For someone who doesn't drink, I had never reeked of alcohol so badly! I was glad to change and enjoy the evening, dancing with beautiful Anna to music by the Police Jazz and Brass Band.

As a gift from the Tanzanian Tourism Board, we received a flight on a small plane to our honeymoon, just the two of us and the pilot. The 30-minute trip took us to the Island Lodge on Mafia Island, not far off the coast from Dar.

I always did my best to control all I could when I was on the track. But life is more important and more complex than what happens in a race. I had known that long before the 1976 boycott, of course, but you can get so focused on the details of everyday decisions and responsibilities that sometimes you have to take a step back and remind yourself that a bigger world exists.

Proposing to Anna, planning the next steps for our growing family together, relaxing away from everybody else for a few days...all of these opportunities reminded us that we were meant to be together. I was with the most important person in the world to me, and we each took care of the other in our own ways. We fulfilled traditional roles for husband and wife in the best of ways. Our union, already grounded in love and respect, was now official for all to see.

///

After missing the Olympics, I made up for lost time with a busy calendar of racing. It wasn't by accident that our wedding took place in October, after the track season was over!

My place in the sport and the sport itself were shifting. I was still only 23 when the 1977 season got underway—still a dangerous competitor, with regular top-three showings both indoors and outdoors. But other runners were emerging onto the scene.

In August 1976, I had placed second by 0.43 seconds in my return to the Emsley Mile, behind 23-year-old David Moorcroft's 3:57.06. In seventh place was 19-year-old Sebastian Coe. A year later, Coe raced by me down the stretch to win his first Emsley Mile. I did not have a single top-10 time in a 1500m in 1977. Moorcroft, Coe, and a third Briton, Steve Ovett, were coming on strong, and John Walker was beating everybody.

Back at Crystal Palace in London on May 18, 1977, a one-tenth of a second victory in the 3000m over Steve Ovett (left) at the Philips Night of Athletics.

Questions about my future were very real. Professional racing wasn't an option. The International Track Association in the United States had folded in 1976. I never gave the ITA serious consideration anyway, because

I wanted to keep my amateur status alive to compete in the Olympics, but its existence shows what a different era it was then.

Most athletes they signed, such as Jim Ryun, Kip Keino, and Ben Jipcho, were late in their careers and had already found success at the Olympics. Prizes were low, just hundreds of dollars. Road races were starting to pop up, but nowhere near the number you see around the world today. Sponsors and media with their corresponding prize money had yet to get on board.

We amateurs had to get by on per-diem expenses. Some athletes made decent money with "under-the-table" payments. I would occasionally hear other runners mention that they had been paid for appearing at a race. But I felt that if I were to ever take money and get banned, I would dishonor myself and my country. My money came from the army, and they gave me time and resources to train. Occasionally, the Tanzanian government would give me gifts for good performances—a wall fan, a bicycle, or a wood carving, for example. They were appreciated, but you don't buy food with a wall fan.

//

I raced everything from 800m to 5000m in preparing for the 1978 Commonwealth Games, hoping to find the right training strategy to defend my world record and 1500m title at the meet. I won 1500s with times above 3:38 that summer. At the All-Africa Games in Algiers, Algeria, I took the victory in a time of 3:36.21. Finally, I felt ready for Edmonton, Canada, where the Commonwealth Games would be held in two weeks.

Just before our final, my teammate Gidamis Shahanga won a gold medal in the marathon. It was a breakthrough performance for him, the first of his many outstanding international marathons over the next 15 years.

Right from the gun I led the way—"Filbert Bayi, putting a statement of intent out immediately," said the BBC announcer. But a long line of runners were close on my heels. I never had more than a step or two

I held the lead in the 1500m final most of the way at the 1978 Commonwealth Games in Edmonton, ahead of Kip Koskei of Kenya (260) and David Moorcroft of Great Britain (center), but Moorcroft caught me on the final straightaway.

lead for the first three laps. There would be no world record today, with a first quarter in 57.67 and a 1:55 at the 800-meter mark. After the bell sounded for the final lap, though, I still thought I had enough left to hold off John Robson of Scotland, who had been right behind me the whole time, Britain's Moorcroft, and Kenya's Wilson Waigwa, who I knew would charge hard from the back of the pack.

Coming out of the final turn, I maintained the lead and Robson and Moorcroft broke from the rest. Down the final straight, Moorcroft slipped past Robson on the outside and then me. I thrust out my torso at the finish in hopes of holding off one Scot on my outside (Robson) and another (Francis Clement) who had snuck on the inside.

Moorcroft ran a great race and took my Commonwealth crown by the slimmest of margins: 3:35.48 to my 3:35.59. Robson was the bronze medalist in 3:35.60, Clement a narrow fourth in 3:35.66, and Waigwa fifth in 3:37.49.

It was my fastest 1500m since I ran on a brand-new track in Zanzibar more than 2½ years earlier. Combined with my gold in Algiers, my silver in Edmonton told me I wasn't done yet.

I was still the world record holder, but young stars were appearing from all over, pacers had begun to show up at European and American meets, and there were rumors of doping from East German athletes and other Eastern bloc countries.

I remember my sprinting teammate Claver Kamanya had bragged about me to a journalist several years earlier: "Bayi is determined and dedicated, even more than Keino. Bayi, he never misses the morning run." He talked about the repeat 200s I would run in 22–23 seconds and repeat 300s I would do in 34–36 seconds in the buildup to the 1974 Commonwealth Games in Christchurch. He said I could beat any 5000m runner in the world, and if I trained, I could run a 46.5 in the 400m. Kamanya should have been my publicist!

Even with that work ethic and commitment, was that enough anymore? My confidence remained high, yet I also could see that I needed to plot out how to stay relevant.

The new year arrived, and little did I know, but one of the most meaningful relationships in my life was on the horizon. As a runner who had figured the sport out as I went along for nearly a decade, who had essentially made my own training and tactical decisions at every step, a person I didn't even know I needed was coming my way: a coach.

1978 COMMONWEALTH GAMES
Commonwealth Stadium, Edmonton, Canada
August 12, 1978

1500m Final

1.	David Moorcroft	ENGLAND	3:35.48
2.	Filbert Bayi	TANZANIA	3:35.59
3.	John Robson	SCOTLAND	3:35.60
4.	Frank Clement	SCOTLAND	3:35.66
5.	Wilson Waigwa	KENYA	3:37.49
6.	Glen Grant	WALES	3:38.05
7.	Richard Tuwei	KENYA	3:40.51
8.	Rod Dixon	NEW ZEALAND	3:41.34
9.	James McGuinness	NORTHERN IRELAND	3:42.59
10.	Tim Hutchings	ENGLAND	3:43.05
11.	Paul Craig	CANADA	3:43.42
12.	Kipsubai Koskei	KENYA	3:45.45

CHAPTER 14

A Coach and a Brother

RON DAVIS WAS IN TANZANIA IN JULY 1976. FOR A TRACK COACH HOPING to land a job in a country he had admired from afar for years, it was the absolute worst time to be there.

When he was in graduate school, studying anthropology at the University of Alberta in Canada in 1973–1974, Davis met African students, including many Tanzanians. He read the influential thinkers who were charting the continent's postcolonial future, especially the writings of Tanzanian president Julius Nyerere and Ghana's first president, Kwame Nkrumah. Nyerere's concept of *ujamaa* resonated with him. The Arusha Declaration of 1967 outlined *ujamaa*, or "familyhood," as a roadmap for Tanzania's socialist future, where its citizens would be unified in building and profiting together for a strong country.

Nyerere had received international attention for his leadership, in which he attempted to transform economic and cultural attitudes among his citizens to think in terms of building national unity and learning to work for both the group and themselves—a blend of communal responsibility and self-reliance. Nyerere wanted Tanzanians to free themselves from the influence from other countries and be satisfied with and proud of what they could achieve as an independent state.

"The Arusha Declaration and our democratic single-party system, together with our national language, Swahili, and a highly politicized and disciplined national army, transformed more than 126 different tribes into a cohesive and stable nation," Nyerere said a few months before he died (Bunting, 1999).

Davis, an American, was disillusioned with the racial strife he experienced as a Black man in his home country. In Canada, he gathered his international friends as often as he could for parties and long discussions about African politics.

He was just as interested in sports as he was social justice, whether supporting civil rights in America or the anti-apartheid movement in Africa. He had received his undergraduate social science degree from San Jose State University, a major center of sport and civil rights activism in the 1960s. As a student-assistant coach, he escorted sprinters Lee Evans, Tommie Smith, and John Carlos to track meets after the 1968 Mexico City Olympics. All were part of the controversial Olympic Project for Human Rights. Smith and Carlos's dramatic medal-stand protest at the 1968 Mexico City Olympics led to death threats in America—and cheers when they ran in Canada. Smith was banned from competing in the United States, but Davis took Carlos and Evans to a meet in Los Angeles.

Davis was a former elite runner himself. He was captain of the 1962 San Jose State University cross country team, which was the first racially integrated national champion squad in that sport in the US. He toured West Africa and northern African countries on a USA goodwill team in 1964, after he narrowly missed making the US Olympic team in the steeplechase. That ignited his curiosity about the continent.

Already impressed with African Olympic gold medalists Keino and Bikila, and Ugandan hurdler John Akii-Bua, Davis was well aware of my February 1974 world record at Christchurch. When he heard what I had done, he said the first words out of his mouth were that it was crazy for someone to be able to set a world record that way.

His semester ended in early 1974, and his Tanzanian friends at school had said they would try to get him hired as a track coach when they returned home. Davis found his own way to Africa, as a teacher at Federal Government College in Sokoto in northern Nigeria. When Nigeria decided to hire African-Americans to revive its national track program, Lee Evans, the 1968 Olympic gold medalist and former 400m world record holder, became the national coach. His first action was to hire Davis, his fellow San Jose State alumnus. The thinking in Nigeria was that these American men had displayed resilience, courage, and determination to find athletic success under difficult conditions. Imagine what they could do as coaches, if given proper resources.

Davis stayed in touch with his Tanzanian friends from the University of Alberta for the next couple years. With the prospect of a boycott looming, the Nigerian National Sports Commission didn't assign him to be one of the coaches to accompany the team to the Montreal Games. (Their delegation returned home immediately after the IOC announced it wouldn't ban New Zealand.) So Davis and his girlfriend decided to go to Tanzania, a country they loved so much that they had named their daughter Tanikka. It was a vacation, but he also hoped to discuss the possibility of coaching the national team with sport administrators while he was there. Davis's friends had told him their contacts had expressed interest in hiring him.

The problem was that they couldn't give him any concrete information. All the key Tanzanian Ministry of Sport personnel were in Mauritius at the time, involved in discussions with the Organization of African Unity about whether to boycott the Olympics. Davis was reading in the *Tanzanian Daily News* all about those discussions. He read about me running a 3:34.8 1500m in Zanzibar and expressing my readiness for the upcoming Olympics. As boycott talks intensified, Davis received a telegram that he was to return to Nigeria immediately. He never got to discuss the possibility of coaching in Tanzania.

By summer 1978, Nigeria's track and field team had become a power. In Algiers, while I was winning the 1500m, the Green and White became the first team to defeat Kenya at the All-Africa Games. Outside the area where athletes were being housed one day, I had just finished a workout and planned to stretch. An athletic-looking man was doing some stretches of his own. We just nodded to each other and continued doing our own thing. Nigeria's coaches were in demand on the continent with their team's performance, but I didn't know who he was. He told me later that he distinctly remembers me walking close to him as he did yoga. He was so shocked he couldn't talk.

Just one week after that historic victory, the Commonwealth Games began in Edmonton, Alberta, Canada. But Nigeria decided not to attend. It was a consistent stance by the country—a protest against participating on the same playing field as New Zealand while New Zealand continued competing with South Africa. Other African countries, including Tanzania, participated.

Though Davis wasn't coaching, he still went to Edmonton, along with Carlos, the controversial American 1968 bronze medalist who was a representative for the shoe company Puma. At the University of Alberta track, I had just finished a 1200m time trial with our team's administrator, Elias Sulus, timing me, so I went for my cooldown.

Davis and Sulus began to chat, and Davis said he would like to coach in Tanzania someday. Sulus replied that the Tanzanian Minister of Culture and Sports was in town. He could arrange a meeting.

Davis and our sports minister, Chediel Mgonja, met a few days later, and soon after the Commonwealth Games ended, the Tanzanian Embassy informed Davis they wanted him to be the new coach of the national team once his responsibilities with Nigeria were fulfilled. By May 1979, the announcement was made public.

A horde of journalists met Davis at the airport in Dar es Salaam. There was a lot of pressure on the new American coach. The country had big expectations for Suleiman Nyambui and me to bring home Tanzania's first Olympic medals. My country expected Davis to do the same for us as he'd done for Nigeria's successful team. I was pretty ambivalent about the whole experience. I had always been independent enough that

I thought I knew how to prepare for the next two years. I didn't expect to get too close to the new guy, no matter what his credentials were.

The Tanzanian officials, meanwhile, were making him feel at home after five-plus years in West Africa. This included Mgonja, Sulus, the head medical doctor Professor Philemon Sarungi, and Erasto Zambi, the ex-sprinter and University of Dar es Salaam coach who helped me in my early days and now was the secretary of the Tanzanian National Olympic Committee.

In May 1979, the top distance runners prepared to convene in Arusha near my home village for altitude training camp. This was a chance for the new coach to get familiar with the team and what would be our home base for international competitions such as the upcoming East Africa Championships in Mombasa, Kenya, and the All-African Championships in Dakar, Senegal.

I worked up a sweat often in summer 1978 as I raced all over Europe, including at the AAA Championships in London. I was fifth in the 5000m, behind Kenya's Henry Rono (first) and my Tanzanian brother, Suleiman Nyambui (fourth).

Davis had just arrived in the country, and I knew I needed to talk with him before the Arusha camp started. I sent word that I wanted to meet with him.

Over tea and sweet biscuits at a restaurant in Dar, I got my first impression of the American—I say that because I had no memory of our two brief previous encounters the year before in Algiers and Edmonton. Davis did. He told me he was starstruck when he was up close to me. I appreciated the honesty, and considering the elite athletes he'd been around in America and Africa, I was a little surprised. He looked athletic, tough, and in charge. I felt good about Mgonja's decision, but I had something more immediate and personal to talk with him about.

It appeared as though he had no idea what was on my mind. I think he was looking for a chance to show me he was the man for the job and that he could help me get ready for Moscow. But I told him that I felt my persistent outbreaks of malaria were further weakening my body and my opportunities to run. I said I was going to be admitted to an infectious diseases hospital in West Germany very soon and that I had no idea when I could resume training.

I can only imagine what he was thinking. He had just uprooted from a job where he was successful and appreciated in order to take a dream assignment in a country he loved. He was to be entrusted to train a world record holder for a shot at Tanzania's first-ever Olympic medal. With barely any time to get his feet on the ground, I'm telling him I am going to be hospitalized and have no timetable to get back on the track. He didn't know if I could ever regain my ability to compete against the best athletes in the world, nor what adjustments he would need to make if I did. He still didn't even know if I was coachable. Welcome to your new job, Ron!

The only positive news I could offer him was my assurance that I would be ready to train in time for the Olympics.

"How can you be so sure? You don't even know when you're going to be able to run again?" he asked me.

I didn't know, but I said it with confidence and great incentive to figure out what was going on with my body. When I had doubts in the past, I was determined to find answers. This time was no different.

"I guess we will have to trust each other," I replied.

CHAPTER 15

Thoughts on Pacing and Malaria

On August 15, 1979, while I lay in a hospital bed, my world record fell. The next morning, I went through my routine tests on the treadmill, measuring oxygen saturation, and had a blood draw when I saw a German newspaper. A photo of a triumphant Sebastian Coe sat below a huge headline. I asked one of the staff to translate it for me, and they confirmed what I suspected: the British phenom had broken my world record.

It happened only about 500 miles south of where I was. While I was at an infectious diseases research hospital in Hamburg, West Germany, recuperating from a series of bouts with malaria and trying to get answers to how I could keep that dreaded disease from recurring, Coe was completing one of the most dominating summers in middle-distance history down in Zurich, Switzerland.

In a span of just 41 days, he broke John Walker's world record in the mile—the one that Walker had taken from me four years ago—erased Alberto Juantorena's two-year-old 800m mark, and now lowered my five-year-old 1500m record as well. My 3:32.16 was now the second-fastest 1500m race of all time, behind Coe's 3:32.03 (ratified as 3:32.1).

//

Coe is still the only person to hold all three of those world marks at the same time, an incredible feat for which he should be applauded.

I've seen Coe often through the years. He's a gentleman, and I give him all due credit. However, I also occasionally bring up the topic of pacing—without bitterness, but I do speak my mind clearly and openly about it.

Pacing became commonplace as race directors realized they could make their event famous by being the site of a world record. For a long time, allowing pacing was frowned upon, but as television and sponsorships made meets more valuable, there was more incentive to look away. The introduction of pacers went against the fundamental rule that all athletes at the starting line must be trying to win. The media, fans, organizers, and athletes allowed it to become the norm. It wasn't long before pacemakers were being hired—and paid extremely well for it. Sometimes now, in a weird twist, rabbits are so good at what they do that they are contractually obligated not to finish the race even if they have the strength to complete it.

The International Amateur Athletic Federation for many years focused on "honest competition." If you're on the track, you're there to finish the race and try to win. That seems a straightforward rule. Obviously, pacers don't fulfill that requirement, and eventually the IAAF dropped it. But, as Pat Butcher wrote in his 2005 book, *The Perfect Distance—Ovett and Coe: The Record-Breaking Rivalry*, the ethical question remains. In his 2004 *Guardian* article, he explicitly blamed the practice on Roger Bannister, who, one year prior to his 1954 four-minute mile, ran with one runner for 2½ laps, then got paced over the next lap by Chris Brasher, who lurked a lap behind awaiting his turn to help:

> The tactic was finessed the following year at the Oxford University AC v AAA match at Iffley Road, and history was made—but at a heavy price. Unfortunately, it has become an indispensable tool for generations of middle-distance runners...
>
> Bannister's run is one of the worst things that ever happened to athletics. Far from being an admirable feat, it was cosy, conniving and dishonest. Its seminal contribution to sport has been to ruin middle-distance running worldwide.

> The worst thing about the first sub-four was the pacemaking. It nurtured the belief that this was the only way to race middle distances—which persists to this day. There's nothing wrong with peers agreeing to pace one another, as long as everyone is trying to win. Paid pacemakers are ruining athletics, because they are effectively being paid to lose. How can this be ethical competition? (Butcher, 2004)

With two world records under his belt, there was intense pressure to find a race where Coe could take a shot at the 1500m mark as well. Organizers promoted the Weltklasse meet in Zurich as a world record opportunity. Kip Koskei of Kenya pushed Coe for about 700 meters before fading dramatically, leaving Coe on his own for the rest of the race. For him to break my record with no one pushing him was remarkable.

In the interview after the race, Coe smiled sheepishly when asked about whether he expected to be challenged more. He said there was "general agreement that we wanted a fast race," though he didn't say by whom. He was asked if he expected Koskei, who took them through 400 meters in 54.2 seconds, to go so fast. He simply said that he didn't tell Koskei to slow down.

Every middle-distance record holder since has benefitted from pacers, including Morocco's Hicham El Guerrouj, who has now held both the mile and 1500m records for more than 20 years. It is a soapbox issue for me and always will be. But I want to be clear that I have great respect for Coe, Ovett (who traded the mile and 1500m world records with Coe throughout the early 1980s), and El Guerrouj. They were brilliant runners and are fine people who, like other elite runners over the past 40-plus years, played by the rules given to them.

It's the nature of athletics that records are made to be broken. But I would say that if you are fortunate enough to set a mark that is the best ever recorded in the history of the world, you recognize the truth of that statement, but on some level you think it will stand the eternal test of time. A record set that is the best ever for a school, a city or a state, a conference, a meet, a country, even a continent, you know someone out there somewhere has already been better and someone else will come along and better yours. The same is not true in the hearts of those who set world records. Intellectually, you know you are only holding the baton until someone else comes along and lowers the time; emotionally, you think maybe the baton is yours to keep.

Achieving a world record should come with a dose of humility and gratitude for all the people and circumstances that helped you get to that point. But there is also a sniff of immortality about it, if you're not careful. When that record falls, you must call on that humility and gratitude again.

That's as it should be. But it doesn't mean it's easy. My state of mind at that time made me feel vulnerable. I was not some retired runner who was ready to congratulate the conqueror, move on, and reflect on my glory days. I was 26 years old and still posting marks that made me someone to notice. Yet, in any world rankings since the 1976 Olympic boycott, I could not deny that I no longer was the clear favorite to be feared in most races I entered. The Walker v. Bayi rivalry had been overtaken by Coe's rivalry with his countryman Ovett as the must-see head-to-head matchup in our sport.

And most concerning of all: as I rested in a Hamburg hospital, far from my family, I realized the Moscow Games were just under 12 months away. I still nurtured dreams of earning that elusive Olympic medal, but I was dealing with the most concerning malaria symptoms of my life.

Malaria was never a problem when I was a child. We were at high-enough altitude that cold temperatures would keep mosquitoes from being too severe. Ever since getting malaria in Dar es Salaam just before my 1973 race in Lagos, though, I had been susceptible from time to time.

In 1978, I contracted it, got better, and then very quickly was infected again. That year, the *New York Times* asked me whether I'd ever be able to run as fast again. "I can't help it," I said. "You say disease, and there is no good result with it. I was sick, I had to stop training, but I am still running. I cannot look back. You must look ahead."

In early 1979, I was concerned and so were the officials in the Tanzanian Ministry of Sport. When I would get fever and fatigue for days at a time, I could not train effectively.

I never fully understood why this was happening. The joke is always that the people who are most sweet are the ones whom mosquitoes are most attracted to. I'm a pretty sweet guy, I suppose, but if I'm being serious, I attribute it at least in part to hard training. Sometimes, when I would push myself in workouts, I would be exhausted and not want to eat afterward. That's when parasites attack—when your body is vulnerable. You need nutrition to repel them. I know a lot of times I didn't force

I was tired and exhausted but looking happy after a workout in Sydney in March 1979. After a brief racing tour in Australia, I barely raced until the fall as I tried to find answers to my constant malaria infections.

myself to eat when I was working hard in training camps. I might even have been hungry, but I didn't want to bother eating. I would just drink water, and nobody else was pushing me to eat.

The West German and Tanzanian governments arranged for me to have an extended stay at a world-renowned tropical diseases research hospital in Hamburg. I was admitted there but also planned to run some races in Europe. For three months, Hamburg would be my home. I'd have regular checkups and my condition would be supervised, but then I could leave for a couple days to run before returning. The reality was that I needed the rest and I ran very sporadically during my time there. In fact, I barely raced during the whole year of 1979.

In late September, I joined the Tanzanian team for altitude training camp in Arusha. They were just coming off a best-ever second-place showing at the East Africa Championships and five medals—also our country's best-ever—at the African Championships. They were running strong. I knew I needed to take it easy, but I also really wanted to be moving again.

//

My very first day back to training in Arusha, Coach Ron Davis and I were jogging. He was a national-class steeplechaser back in the day; in 1964, he made it to the finals at the US Olympic Trials. He still kept himself in good shape, but that was 15 years ago. I didn't mind taking it easy for a few miles and chatting with him at his pace. At some point, though, he said not to hold back if I wanted to go. I was feeling good and did just that. He said later, "I'd never seen a runner take off and disappear the way he did. I was in shock. All I could think about was, Wow! No wonder this man had the world records in the mile and 1500. Welcome to Mr. Filbert Bayi!"

This was my first extended time with Davis, and he said he was immediately impressed with my humility and respect toward him. He once wrote:

> From the very first day of training until I departed Tanzania, we never had any disagreement or tension in our relationship. Filbert was the ideal athlete and it was a joy working with him. He accepted my advice and training methods without even a hint of resistance. My anxieties about training a world class runner faded quickly in large part because of Filbert's attitude and willingness to work hard and to listen. In reality I didn't have to do a lot or to make any major adjustments to Filbert's running style or approach to running. He was a gifted athlete whose only desire was to excel. I tried to incorporate all that I had learned from my previous coaches and others who had success in training distance runners. Incorporating strength training when we could along with speed and sprint techniques I learned from the great Bud Winter were the foundation of my philosophy for coaching. I approached our training like you would train for a marathon with hill training and distance for speed and endurance. The good thing about this approach was that the athletes, including Bayi, were already acclimated to hill training so this was very easy to implement. (Davis, 2016)

I wouldn't go *quite* that far. We had typical training disagreements, but always respectful ones and never over anything substantial. The biggest issue was getting on the same page some days about when to rest and when to push the gas. What I appreciated about his approach was that he talked with athletes to see how we were feeling. From what I observed when I saw coaches interact with their athletes at meets, I don't believe that was the philosophy for many coaches of that era.

He didn't try to be a dictator or pile on miles. He knew when we were tired, and when we were tired he made sure we got rest and recovered from the hard training so we were ready for the next day. Probably more often, he'd say we were done for the workout, and I'd say I needed to go farther or do a few more reps. He'd listen to me most of the time then too. I was not lazy, and neither were my teammates.

At least twice a week, we ran up a hill that he named MGM…Mount Gold Medal. It was about 300 meters long—sprinters would run repeats up it and the distance runners would go up and down it for as long as an hour. When I did tempo runs headed down the dirt road to the Arusha highway, others checked their watches to see how fast they were going. I just kept striding as though my body had its own clock.

Davis said that we African runners were focused, disciplined, and determined. We were always on time for practice, and we were passionate about our training. He didn't have to try to use head games to motivate us as he said was sometimes the case with his American athletes.

Our partnership was strong, our friendship was growing, and our trust was quickly building.

Davis gave me a 1200m time trial that I ran in 2:54, ahead of several other young runners he invited who also went sub-3:00. One of those was Jimmy Igohe, who reached the 1500m semifinals at the 1984 Olympics.

After that test, I clocked a 3:38.3 in the 1500m at a meet in Zanzibar on Christmas Day. That seemed like a good omen heading into a critical Olympic year. Davis was even more thrilled:

> When I saw him win the 3:38 in Zanzibar and how easy he ran the race alone, I thought to myself at that time, "Ron, keep training him because Filbert knows what he has to do in a race." I never gave Filbert any advice on how to run a race because he had a history of knowing what to do without a coach when he broke the world records.
>
> The officials were hesitant to invite Filbert for indoor competition in America because they did not think he was in shape the way he was in previous years. When I sent the Zanzibar results to Paul Poce, whom I was communicating with from Toronto, he quickly wrote back saying Filbert would be invited to the 1980 indoor meets in Canada and the United States.

This was important. I was far from being in Olympic shape, and the only way to get back there was to test myself against the best racers in the world, who would be in those North American indoor meets. Though my results over the past four years had been uneven, I still had the same confidence in my ability to train hard and race smart as my coach did. That sustained me as I prepared for the 1980 season.

People would always ask me how I pushed my body so much in workouts. I didn't have an answer for them other than, "It hurts." If you don't hurt in practice, you're not going to be willing to hurt in races. If you hurt in practice, you'll be prepared when you're hurting and getting pushed in a race. It really is that simple. Were people looking for a more complicated answer?

Even when you're in shape, maybe 80 percent of a workout is comfortable. It's the other 20 percent that counts though. How you respond when it hurts determines how successful you can be. Make no mistake about it...you can't avoid that 20 percent. If you're a human being, it's going to hurt.

CHAPTER 16

Clearing a Hurdle in Moscow

WE ARRIVED IN TORONTO UNPREPARED FOR JUST HOW COLD IT would be. The American sprinter John Carlos was working for Puma at the time, and he was in town for the meet. He went to a Puma outlet to get his old friend Ron Davis and Ron's Tanzanian team additional hooded sweatshirts, sweatpants, and gloves.

On one morning run on snowy roads in frigid downtown Toronto, I remember a bank clock on Yonge Street reading minus 20 degrees Celsius. The hotel sauna and whirlpool felt so good as we thawed out after that outdoor run.

At Maple Leaf Gardens there, I placed third in 4:00.2 behind Eamonn Coghlan and Wilson Waigwa. The next night in Ottawa, I was second (4:01.7) behind Coghlan. A week later in Winnipeg, I was near world-record pace through the 1320-meter mark and held on to win in 3:58.6, ahead of Waigwa and my Princeton host, Craig Masback.

I ran a mile at the Sunkist Invitational in Los Angeles in 3:54.5—faster than any indoor time I had ever run in that event and the fifth-fastest indoor time ever. I placed third behind Eamonn Coghlan (3:52.9, just three-tenths of a second off his indoor world record) and Steve Scott (3:53.0, the third-fastest indoor time ever).

I set another indoor PR in the 3000m in Edmonton with a time of 7:50.4, even beating my friend Suleiman Nyambui.

At the Jack in the Box mile in San Diego, I ran 3:55.5 and beat Coghlan, John Walker, Scott, and Thomas Wessinghage of West Germany.

My six indoor performances in 1980 had me feeling young. If I wasn't as dominant now as I was five years ago, I had moments that were as good as or better than my 1975 tour of the US—and I was doing this on virtually no speedwork. Most runners aren't in top shape during the early season, especially in an Olympic year. Still, I was aware of how far back I had fallen since the previous summer. These showings made me believe that with the proper work I could be competitive in Moscow.

My training plan during my time in North America included 8x400m repeats on Tuesdays, long afternoon runs of an hour or more on Mondays and Wednesdays, and 8x200m repeats on Thursdays unless the race was on a Friday, in which case I'd go for a 45-minute to an hour run. In addition, I did an hour-long run most mornings.

A big topic of conversation at that time was the threat of a US-led boycott of the Olympics that summer. US President Jimmy Carter had announced that possibility just weeks before I arrived in his country, as a response to the recent Soviet invasion of Afghanistan. Carter even sent Muhammad Ali to tour five African countries on a diplomatic mission to join the boycott.

Ali started in Tanzania, but when he landed in Dar es Salaam, President Julius Nyerere refused to meet the boxing champion. Chediel Mgonja, our minister of youth and culture, spent time with Ali, but Tanzania's position never wavered. When Africa asked for support for its boycott over massacred South African schoolchildren in 1976, the United States wasn't interested. Now, in a battle between two superpowers about territorial expansion, Ali was asking for support from a continent that had been a pawn for centuries until the very recent past. I made that argument in numerous interviews while I was in North America, including the "Good Morning, Canada" TV show where I appeared with Flora MacDonald, Canada's Secretary of State for External Affairs.

As spring neared, running for my country in Moscow was my focus–not worrying about which countries were going to be there.

//

We returned to high altitude for training camp. For a little variety, we stayed east of Arusha in the city of Moshi. I was feeling healthy again, and any doubts I had about putting my workouts into the hands of somebody else soon dissipated. Davis had been successful as an athlete and as a coach. He had a calm yet firm demeanor with everyone he encountered, whether up-and-coming athletes or sport administrators who held the money for the team to train and travel.

He was deferential to me from the outset, figuring I had earned some slack if I wanted it. But pretty much immediately, I realized I didn't want it. Yes, I had found success, mostly on my own. I believed in myself as much as I did when I was breaking world records and willing myself to the front of the pack. But I knew as I got older that I could benefit from a coach with extensive experience and knowledge.

I had received endless support from Werner Kramer before he returned to East Germany. Erasto Zambi was giving of his time; Elias Sulus, too. They would discuss workouts with me, clock me on the track, take care of travel arrangements, and offer whatever they could. For all of that, I was grateful. But they were always relying on my advice. Rather than expecting a coach to develop my racing fitness then, I was basing my workouts on how my body felt and what I picked up from reading track and field magazines and sport science journals.

Davis had studied exercise physiology extensively. He was curious and asked questions whenever he came across coaches at meets. He ran for and coached beside some of the greatest running minds in the world at San Jose State, home of Bud Winter's famous "Speed City" sprinting crew.

When Davis took over the reins of the Tanzanian national team, I saw that he wanted to train people who were committed and weren't lazy. I was an eager student. Davis became my first real coach.

The first true interval workout I ever did under Davis was repeat 200s at the University of Toronto indoor track in 1980. Davis was always careful to rein me in that year. He felt I was a high-quality engine and he couldn't afford for me to get injured and not make it to the starting line at the Olympics.

Moshi did not have a track to train on, so Davis did a lot of improvising. He'd have me run with the middle-distance runners early in the workout, but then he'd bring in the 400-meter runners for the final reps and require me to keep pace with those fast guys when I was already fatigued. For years, my speed had been considered a vulnerable spot for me, but sessions like that gave me confidence that I could still compete against the best down the stretch.

Another session would have Davis standing on a golf course where we were doing a fartlek workout. Davis was situated on a small plateau, but he looked like Moses on Mt. Sinai. Davis's whistle could be heard by every runner no matter how far away. Fartleks allow distance runners to work on intermittent surging and maintaining a fast pace. Unlike a track workout, you don't know precisely what the splits are. It's an ideal way to combine speed and endurance training. When you master fartlek training, you learn how to destroy your competition.

It really wasn't much different from the makeshift fartlek workouts I did chasing buses on the streets of Dar as a teenager. Training in these conditions was fun, like a game, full of surprises and often intensely competitive.

We had many runners at our training camp hoping to make an impression and earn a spot on the Olympic team. Once, a young, fearless runner named Leogard Martin decided to challenge me on a hill workout. I didn't like having anyone in front of me during training any more than I did in races, so I kept fighting him off. After I got back to the hostel where we were staying, I collapsed and had to be taken to the hospital. I was simply exhausted, they said, and they released me.

We had so many runners that Davis would hold all-comers meets a couple times a month at the facilities in Arusha. This gave me a chance to race different distances. I'd run a 10,000m time trial at high altitude one night and anchor a 4x400m relay leg a couple weeks later.

Moshi was 80 kilometers (50 miles) east of Arusha. It was directly south of Mount Kilimanjaro about 30 kilometers (18 miles) so on long weekend runs, we could clearly see the majestic peak, always it seemed under a deep-blue sky.

//

Summer came, and I felt as healthy and confident as I had in at least two years. The combination of endurance and hill training, speed workouts, and sprinting technique were kicking in. I was fit enough to race a lot without the fatigue my body was constantly dealing with the year before.

I actually posted my best performances ever in three events. I placed third in a two-mile at the Talbot Games in London on June 27. It was a personal best of 8:19.45, less than a second behind Dave Moorcroft and Nat Muir from Great Britain. The Bislett Games in Oslo were held on July 1. I was third in the 3000m with a PR and national record of 7:39.27. Two weeks later, back in Oslo, I ran another PR in the 5000m in 13:18.2. My second-place finish was just three-tenths of a second behind Muir and just ahead of Nyambui in one of the fastest 5000s in the world that year.

In between, I was on world-record pace through 1200 meters in a more familiar race—the 1500m at Göteborg, Sweden. The crowd was on its feet, exhorting me, but I settled for a winning time of 3:36.97 and the Most Outstanding Athlete award for the meet. A distant second was Poland's Bronisław Malinowski, the steeplechase silver medalist in Montreal in 1976.

Davis had me competing in longer events, in part as a recognition that my speed had diminished. I might need to consider a different path to an Olympic gold medal rather than go against the young world record holders Coe and Ovett in the 800m and 1500m. To punctuate that point, on the same day and same Bislett Stadium track where I ran the 3000m, Ovett broke Coe's world record in the mile with a 3:48.8.

I remembered Rod Dixon saying after I broke the world record in Christchurch that if John Walker and I were the future of the 1500m, then he'd better start looking at the 5000m for himself. He was just 23 when he said that. I was 27 years old now and realized what it was like to be in his shoes.

The American-led boycott was keeping many great athletes home from the Olympics, but Great Britain still planned to be in Moscow.

With the Olympics looming in late July, my coach and I had a crucial question to answer—which event should I run? If the 800m and 1500m were off the table, I thought that left the 3000m and 5000m, and I liked my chances in either. Davis had other ideas though. We sat down to discuss it in early May.

"What about the steeplechase?" Davis asked.

To say I wasn't experienced in the 3000m steeplechase would be an understatement. I had a DNF in the East and Central Africa Championships in Lusaka, Zambia, back in 1971. Then there was the Munich Olympic heat that didn't go so well, and a 1973 time trial in Arusha. In 1978, I did the steeplechase at the Army Games in Dar as a little experiment. I saw a photo of me in the local paper and it looked like I was running a high jump or something. There was so much air between my legs and the hurdles; those hurdles did not budge and I didn't want to take a chance on hitting one wrong. I had to sprint between the hurdles to make up lost time, which I could do two years ago. But I would get destroyed if I tried that in the Olympics.

That was the extent of my steeplechasing through the years. In addition to an inefficient hurdling technique, I was small. I might be agile, but it was easy for me to get knocked around. Even if we did commit to it, the quirky event wasn't even scheduled for every meet. I would have few opportunities for an Olympic dress rehearsal.

I was clear about my concerns to my coach, but Davis did his best to sell me on the idea. He thought if I could have two months of solid training, then a medal was possible against the field expected to line up in Moscow. He said I had the gift of vision and intelligence to figure out how to race most effectively. Most of the great middle-distance runners of the past 15–20 years had full-time coaches, he said, and I did it pretty much alone and had been overwhelmingly successful. Davis also reminded me that the great Kip Keino entered the 1972 Olympic steeplechase final with hardly any experience and the slowest time in the field, yet came away with gold.

I was open to the suggestion, but after a few hurdling workouts my confidence stayed low. I won a race in Arusha, but in a time of 8:45.0 that would be unlikely to advance me beyond the first heat in the Olympics.

I decided to call Davis's bluff. I promised him if I ran under 8:20 in the steeplechase in any competition in Europe, then I would change my event at the Olympics to the steeplechase.

My opportunity to do that came at the DN Galan meet at Stockholm, Sweden, on July 8, less than three weeks before the track and field sessions began in Moscow. I surprised myself with a victory in 8:17.98, the world's best time to date that year and a Tanzanian record. More importantly at the time, it was nearly three full seconds ahead of Poland's Malinowski, who was considered the event favorite for the upcoming Olympics. In short order, Davis sent a telex to the Tanzania National Olympic Committee requesting that they enter me into the 3000m steeplechase for Moscow.

An even bigger surprise came when Edwin Moses offered to help me with my hurdling technique, which is a little like Muhammad Ali offering tips on a left hook or Diana Ross asking if you would sing a duet with her. Moses was in Sweden to win the 400m hurdles, something the American world record holder did an astonishing 122 consecutive races over almost 10 full years from 1977 through 1987. Unfortunately, Moses would not be able to defend his Olympic title because of his country's boycott. He and Davis had become friends after meeting at the Talbot Games in London, and he was willing to help me out. The next morning he gave me some pointers, which further boosted my confidence. I wasn't going to make a career out of hurdling after one session with the greatest hurdler of all time, but, I thought, it might just give me enough of an edge to win a gold medal.

//

Despite the boycott of 65 countries, Moscow felt like a giant festival. The Soviet Union wanted to be a showcase for socialism to the world that was still tuning in. I received a lot of attention, since I was a world record holder chasing an elusive medal after missing the 1976 Olympics. I was still signed up to run the 1500m and the steeplechase, so there was speculation about whether I could match Kip Keino's 1972 two medals in those events. Also, my coach was the only American in the Athletes Village, which made for an intriguing storyline in those Cold War days.

I won the first heat of the steeplechase in Moscow on July 26, 1980, to advance to the semifinals.

With the journalists' constant questions, Tanzanian officials wisely placed Coach Davis, 5000m runner Nyambui, and me in a large three-bedroom suite in the Village away from other athletes. Our delegation consisted of 41 athletes, much larger than the group of 15 Tanzanians who were at the last Olympics we attended, in 1972.

I decided to withdraw from the 1500m and focus just on the steeplechase. I won the opening heat with a time of 8:21.38, just ahead of Eshetu Tura of Ethiopia. In the semifinals, I edged Tura again, this time by six-hundredths of a second in 8:16.11. Malinowski won the other semifinal in 8:21.15 after an opening-heat win of 8:29.8.

I was impressed that I had already lowered my PR from Stockholm in a qualifying round, but I knew Malinowski and Tura would be tough to beat in the final. Malinowski was experienced, with a runner-up showing in Montreal four years earlier and two European Championships golds in 1974 and 1978. And, relatively speaking, based on his first two races in Moscow, the stocky 29-year-old Pole was well rested.

I wanted desperately to win a gold medal for Tanzania, so whatever spectacle the Olympics was to others, I treated it as all business. Considering where I was at now compared to one year earlier, I was grateful to be in this position, but I also didn't want to jeopardize the opportunity, since I knew how rare they were. The world was watching, and the citizens of my 20-year-old nation were expecting me to deliver Tanzania's first ever Olympic medal.

I wanted to shut out all distractions and draw on my inner strength to complete the task at hand. So to conserve my energy, I basically stopped speaking. To the outside world, I can come across as distant, but people who know me well, like my coach and teammates, thought this was unusual behavior. Davis worried that I was becoming too withdrawn and was concerned something was bothering me. I was so focused that I don't think I gave him enough of a response to put his mind at ease. On the morning of the finals, as we entered Luzhniki Stadium, I put my arms around him and told him softly, "Don't worry. Everything is going to be OK." I smiled and Davis flashed back a huge, relieved grin.

When the gun sounded, I immediately went to the front to limit the potential for getting spiked and to keep Malinowski from getting comfortable. It had been eight years since my last Olympics, and while I had hundreds of races under my belt since then, I could count all my steeplechases during that time on one hand. How strange to be so experienced and such a novice all at the same time in an Olympic final.

Tura went with me, and for two-plus laps he was right on my tail. Finally, I started to open up a gap on him and he put a gap between himself and the rest of the field. Soon after the halfway mark, I had a 20-yard lead on him and I was near world record pace. But I was tiring.

My hurdling was much improved, but I was losing speed on my landing more than I would have liked rather than gliding forward.

With a lap and a half to go, Malinowski caught Tura, but I still maintained a consistent four-second lead on the second position, as I had for nearly a mile. I was at just under seven minutes as the bell lap sounded—still below the pace of Kenya's Henry Rono when he ran an 8:05.4 to set the world record in 1978. But Malinowski was gaining ground fast.

I heard him just a step behind me as I launched myself over the hurdle before the final water jump. I turned to look over my left shoulder as we rounded the last curve. He rolled past me on the right. When I planted my right foot in the water for the last time, it stuck in the pit hard and I almost stood upright. My muscles were spent, and it showed in my landing. I managed to stay on my feet, but I knew I wasn't going to reel him back.

My form on the 35th and final hurdle was awful, as I had to stutter-step to propel myself over it. It felt like I was climbing the hurdle. My only goal was to just get over it safely so I could sprint to the finish and hold off Tura.

I did that, by one second. I had achieved Tanzania's first Olympic medal—a silver—with a new national record of 8:12.48, nearly three seconds behind Malinowski. We shook hands and hugged, and congratulated each other in English.

I was led to the postrace drug-testing room with the other runners, still exhausted and thinking about what I had accomplished. Gold was my goal, but I never saw myself as having failed to reach it, mostly I believe because I knew I could not have done any more on that day. The Pole had run a smart tactical race. He maintained a steady pace and caught me when I had nothing left to expend. He deserved to be an Olympic champion, and I felt I had accomplished something that would make my country proud, just as John Akhwari had in 1968.

We emerged for the medal ceremony. Yes, hearing the Tanzanian national anthem, "Mungu ibariki Afrika" (which is Swahili for "God bless Africa"), would have been wonderful, but as I stood on the podium listening to the Polish anthem, watching the Polish, Ethiopian, and Tanzanian flags waving in the breeze, I felt relaxed and content.

I led the pack almost the whole way of the steeplechase final on July 31, 1980, at Luzhniki Stadium. Eshetu Tura (187) of Ethiopia was on my heels much of the race and earned a bronze medal.

When we stepped down and were led out of the stadium by Russian women in their traditional dresses, I smiled at no one in particular, strolled off the track, and just enjoyed the moment, happy for Tanzania. I'm a driven person, always looking to the next goal. It's easy sometimes to forget to breathe in all that life offers, the challenges and celebrations, the obstacles we overcome, the connections we make.

We mustn't forget to take in the joy when it comes to us. Those meaningful moments stand out, but they don't stand still. They give way to new responsibilities and crises that arrive quickly and demand our attention.

Before we left Moscow, my friend and countryman Suleiman Nyambui earned a silver medal in the 5000m, six-tenths of a second behind Ethiopia's legendary Miruts Yifter, giving Tanzania two Olympic medals and hope that we could add to that total in the years ahead. But that didn't happen. As I write this in 2022, our two silvers remain Tanzania's only Olympic medals.

Furthermore, just over a year later, Malinowski was tragically killed in a car accident at age 30. And my coach left to coach in neighboring Mozambique.

But I didn't know all of that then. Those two incidents, both out of my control, show that change is always around the corner. Meaningful experiences in our lives, whether celebrations or losses, become memories we draw on later for inspiration as we move forward. At that particular moment in 1980, all I could say with certainty was that Coach Davis and I had cleared the hurdle and won a medal for the country we both proudly represented.

1980 OLYMPIC GAMES

Luzhniki Stadium, Moscow, Soviet Union
July 31, 1980

3000m Steeplechase Final

1.	Bronisław Malinowski	POLAND	8:09.7	
2.	Filbert Bayi	TANZANIA	8:12.48	NR
3.	Eshetu Tura	ETHIOPIA	8:13.57	
4.	Domingo Ramón	SPAIN	8:15.74	
5.	Francisco Sánchez	SPAIN	8:17.93	
6.	Giuseppe Gerbi	ITALY	8:18.47	PR
7.	Bogusław Mamiński	POLAND	8:19.43	
8.	Anatoliy Dimov	SOVIET UNION	8:19.75	
9.	Vasile Bichea	ROMANIA	8:23.86	
10.	Dušan Moravčík	CZECHOSLOVAKIA	8:29.03	
11.	Lahcen Babaci	ALGERIA	8:31.8	
12.	Tommy Ekblom	FINLAND	8:40.86	

Bronisław Malinowski caught me just before the final water jump to take gold while I earned Tanzania's first-ever Olympic medal.

PART THREE

Chasing a Legacy

Filbert Bayi Schools, Kimara, Tanzania, 2019.

CHAPTER 17

A Treasure in My Travel Bag

Returning home to Tanzania after the Olympics in 1980, I had one silver medal in my bag but many different directions that my life could go.

At 27 years old, I was long past being a young underdog, but I felt sure I wasn't done yet either. I still had plenty of races ahead of me—maybe even a gold medal in four years at the Los Angeles Games in the steeplechase or a longer distance. Or perhaps I should lose my amateur status and do the road races that were starting to become popular and offered prize money.

Coming off of the Olympics, everybody was running a lot. The Western athletes who weren't able to compete in Moscow wanted to salvage their seasons, and those of us who did run at the Olympics were chasing any opportunity to make the most of our fitness.

I raced nine times in 18 days and saw many of the same guys all around Europe: Budapest, Brussels, London…we were everywhere. My performances were adequate: miles in the 3:55–3:57 range but off the podium; three wins in the 3000m, in Innsbruck, Malmö, and Luxembourg. It was hard to stay consistent when we were running that often. All of us felt that.

I enjoyed getting to see my countryman Zakaria Barie improve dramatically with so much racing. He ran a 13:29.47 in the 5000m in

Dublin that was much better than his Olympic heats, showing he was ready to be a world-class athlete for Tanzania.

Two races in Switzerland just two weeks after my Moscow medal reminded me that I needed to look at longer distances. At the Zurich Weltklasse meet, I placed sixth in the 1500m in 3:35.87. Sebastian Coe was trying to lower his world record of 3:32.1 that he'd set one year earlier on that same track. He came up just short in 3:32.19, but what stands out in my mind was how we were told at the starting line not to interfere with the pacer and Coe. Two nights later at the Lausanne Athletissima, I placed eighth in the 800m in 1:49.85.

Times had changed, in the sport and for me.

I saw Craig Masback, the American who once had me taking every turn in New Jersey, at the hotel in one of those cities. He had a small box, about the size of a paperback novel, with thin cords hanging from it that connected to foam circles on his ears. When I asked him about it, he said it was the latest technology from Japan. He was listening to audiocassettes through it. I had never seen headphones so small and portable. Masback said I could have it, a very kind gesture that made me one of the first owners of a Walkman on the track circuit. This was much more convenient than buying vinyl records in Kingston or New York to listen to my music!

Times had definitely changed.

I tried something completely different two months later. Ron Davis had suggested it way back in the summer. He said my smooth tempo on two-hour runs in the hills of Moshi and the mountains of Arusha would be ideal for a marathon. Besides, training for it would be good endurance work for whatever I did in the future.

We traveled to New York City in October. The first day we were there, I stepped in a hole in Central Park and severely turned my ankle. There was no fracture, according to the sports medicine staff, but I had trouble walking. I boarded the bus to the start line on race day not sure how it would go. It was not easy. I finished the New York City Marathon 36th in 2 hours, 20 minutes, 34 seconds, almost 11 minutes behind the leaders. I wasn't all that excited about signing up for another one.

Somewhere between a half mile and 26.2 miles, I needed to find the next chapter of my running life.

//

One thing I knew for certain was that my decisions needed to put my family first. Our son was now 5 years old. Whether it was the indoor season in the United States in winter or the outdoor season in Europe in summer, being apart from my family so often was difficult. I received my captain's salary, and the army was generous in giving me time to train, but financially these were not easy times. My wife, Anna, was resilient and independent. When I was traveling, she took care of Engelbert while also managing a hair salon, a poultry business in which she sold meat and eggs to local groceries and individuals, and a distribution business where she transported prawns to Botswana and South Africa.

We were always a good team—practical in finding creative solutions and respectful of each other's contributions to the marriage. Those early years set the stage for many future collaborations that only increased in scope and drew us closer together.

My collaboration with Davis, so successful in preparing for the Olympics, ended sooner than I had expected. Davis had been heavily involved in African politics since he arrived on the continent from the US. He believed, as did I, that sports offers opportunities for healing and unity that other segments of society could not. Given the opportunity in 1981 to be the national track coach in neighboring Mozambique, he decided to take it. Despite internal doubts about his decision, he felt he would be in a better position to contribute to the struggle against apartheid in the newly independent country of Mozambique, which bordered South Africa.

Davis told me that concerns about injuring me after I came back from the tropical diseases hospital in West Germany had kept him from prescribing too much speedwork in the runup to Moscow. With several years to adhere to a proper training schedule leading up to Los Angeles, we both had high hopes for another medal at a distance somewhere between 3000 and 10,000m.

"I had tears when I boarded the plane to Mozambique and questions were circulating in my mind if I had made the correct decision," Davis said in 2019. "I felt I was going to make a contribution to the struggle to liberate South Africa, not realizing how much love I had for Tanzania and the athletes. If I had stayed, I think I would have made a major impact with the athletes in the 1984 Olympics."

I never blamed him for his decision. We both had much to do in the years ahead that we thought was important, and you should never stand in somebody's way when they have good intentions and purpose behind their goals. As it turned out, over the next decade much of my work would be in his home country, while much of his work would be among my African brothers and sisters.

//

Throughout the 1970s, I had little doubt that my service to my country was as an army technician and a top-level runner. I really didn't even think I could go to college because of my military obligation. Getting an education was very important to me, but I liked the men I worked with and believed in our mission. I had no reason to complain. Still, as I got a little older, I began to think more deeply about what service could mean.

Way back in 1974, Kenyan Mike Boit, who placed sixth in my world record 1500m that year, introduced me to Bill Silverberg, then the coach at Eastern New Mexico University. African athletes were beginning to be recruited by American coaches, and Silverberg was at the forefront. He invited me to join Boit at ENMU, but I had made a commitment to the military. The time wasn't right to pursue higher education.

By 1982, I felt the pull of returning to school at the same time that Anna was pregnant with our second child. When our daughter, Annette, was born, the thought of leaving the country was all the more difficult. But Anna was supportive of my going to the United States. It was a sacrifice we were both willing to make. We felt my getting a college degree was the best decision for the family, and a scholarship from an American university was the most appealing long-term solution.

Boit and others were an inspiration to me. He had received a bachelor's degree from ENMU and two master's degrees from Stanford University. Soon, he would begin a doctor of education degree program at the University of Oregon. I asked the Tanzanian Army for a four-year leave and sought out Silverberg, who then was an assistant at the University of Oklahoma (OU), to see if a scholarship was available.

"Bill Silverberg promised me the one thing I desperately wanted: A good education," I told the *Daily Oklahoman*. "With that, I will be able to take better care of my family—my mother, my eight sisters and brothers, and my wife and two children" (Perovich, 1982).

I had to take an English comprehension test that summer, which was required for all international students at OU. That was the easy part. For months, officials at OU and my small school in Karatu were in correspondence. I had last attended classes there in 1970, and I'd left for the army before the school year was over, which I'm sure added to the confusion. They were slow to respond to the American university's need to verify my academic credentials. Eventually, they had provided all the original transcripts and papers from my time there except one. They sent a copy, but that wasn't sufficient. Without the original, the cross country season got underway and I still had not signed an NCAA letter of intent, though I did begin taking courses. But I was not officially a freshman on the Sooner varsity cross country team.

When I finally got a chance to compete in October, I was 29 years old and likely the oldest track athlete in the country. Certainly I was one of the most scrutinized. It wasn't just because of my world records and Olympic medal; it was because of the debate then raging in American collegiate sports about international athletes—especially Africans—competing with American-born athletes for scholarships.

The issue was particularly hot at the University of Texas at El Paso, which won 17 national titles in cross country and indoor and outdoor track and field between 1974 and 1981 under coach Ted Banks. Many of his best were African distance runners, including my fellow Tanzanians Suleiman Nyambui, Zakariah Barie, and Gidamis Shahanga. UTEP was called the "Foreign Legion," and not affectionately by coaches getting trounced by the Miners.

Largely because of Banks's success in recruiting older African runners, the NCAA installed an age requirement saying that an athlete over age 20 loses a year of eligibility each year thereafter. It was called "the Banks Rule" by some, also not affectionately. However, that rule included a clause that said years spent in the military or as a church missionary didn't count. Since I had been in the Tanzanian Army since my late teens, I was eligible to compete once my final paper came through.

When it did, the season was nearly over and I was dealing with a pulled groin muscle. I enjoyed my classes and could keep up with them well. I planned on getting a sports administration degree. My English had improved immensely since I first started being interviewed in the mid-1970s, and I was well aware of fitness principles and exercise physiology from a decade of high-level training. However, the adjustment was more difficult than I had anticipated. I did not like the setting of Norman, Oklahoma, for running. All autumn long, it was a damp cold that I never got used to and I'm sure was a contributing factor to my groin troubles. And all that thunder and lightning! The flat-as-a-tabletop setting was not conducive to the training I most enjoyed, the hills and altitude in northern Tanzania. It wasn't OU's fault, but I never could get comfortable there.

I called Nyambui.

"Filbert, you're lonely," he said. "Come join us in El Paso. We will move you."

//

El Paso, Texas, sits just over the Rio Grande Rift from Mexico at 3,740 feet elevation, and the nearby Franklin Mountains provide peaks well over a mile high. It's in the Chihuahuan Desert, with mild winters and hot summers, and is home to about 800,000 people. Arusha, near the southern portion of the Great African Rift, is the largest city in northern Tanzania at about half a million people. Arusha is 4,593 feet high, with mountains (including Kilimanjaro) that point well over 10,000 feet into the air.

Is it any wonder Tanzanians loved to train in El Paso? The only difference was that the mountains back home were lush and green, while those in West Texas were brown and bald.

Banks came up with his plan to recruit Africans to run for UTEP soon after he arrived in 1973. "As Banks began his new job, he quickly found that his California contacts weren't going to help him at UTEP," *Runner's World* wrote about him. "As a result and as the year went on, he had little to show for his recruiting efforts. Like all desert-dwellers, he was going to have to adapt to survive" (Leivers, 2012).

ENMU had several Kenyans on their squad who came to El Paso to train during spring break. Banks talked with some of them and a few contacts he had in Africa. A Kenyan runner named Wilson Waigwa heard about Banks and wrote to say he'd like to run for UTEP, if there was a spot for him. Banks didn't really know what to expect, but he invited Waigwa to join the team. Immediately, the Kenyan was crushing the returning Miner runners.

The pipeline was established and continued throughout Banks's tenure, which ended in February 1982 when he became Converse's national director of running promotions. He went on to develop the company's first line of track and field shoes.

I had talked with Nyambui about transferring to UTEP as the 1983–1984 school year neared, and he talked with the new coach, Larry Heidebrecht, about me. Nyambui had finished his eligibility, but he stayed in town to coach. Barie, Shahanga, and Mohamed Rutiginga were still competing at the university, and all of us loved the idea of being in the same place for training. It could be like Arusha or Moshi all over again.

On my way from Tanzania to El Paso in September 1983, I stopped in Norman to tell Oklahoma coach J.D. Martin I wouldn't be returning. I needed to tell him in person and apologize for leaving on short notice. It was difficult, but I knew it was the best decision for me.

The first-ever World Championships in athletics had been held in Helsinki in August 1983, and Tanzania's small contingent had failed to medal. Nyambui and I were injured. Shahanga was fifth and Barie didn't make the final in the 10,000m. Agapius Masong was fifth and Juma Ikangaa 15th in the marathon.

The thinking was that if we Tanzanians worked out together, we could be in good shape for the Olympics in a year. I had to sit out the 1983–1984 season after transferring from OU, after which I'd have three years of eligibility left. That meant I could still take classes and train with friends I knew in a location that suited me. Things were lining up nicely for my LA tune-up.

//

My Tanzanian brothers were happy to greet me in El Paso. They had dominated the college competition, and now we had expectations of continuing the momentum from the 1980 Olympics. There were so many great runners during the Banks era, but my brother Nyambui stood above them all. Nyambui encouraged me to help him lead the young Tanzanians.

I knew how good he was when I trained with him back in the early '70s, and he remembered how I mentored him until he could keep up with me—even though I fought as hard as I could to not let him pass me…ever. Nyambui reminded me of how focused we were on doing the workouts we devised together. We cheered for each other and if one of us lost, we would go back to our hotel room and tell the other how we would make sure to not let that happen the next time.

Nyambui was a factor in my setting the world record in 1975. He has an amazing story of his own. In addition to becoming one of the best distance runners in the world in the '70s, he joined the Tanzania National Service and taught math before enrolling at UTEP.

Nyambui was 29 when he completed his eligibility in 1982, having won four straight NCAA titles at 10,000m, three NCAA titles at 5000m, and the 1980 individual cross country championship. During that time, he of course won Olympic silver at 5000m and broke the world indoor 5000m record, at the Millrose Games in 13:20.4.

He was part of UTEP's legendary 1981 cross country championship. It was the school's sixth in seven years, and with Banks leaving just a few months later, it turned out to be a nearly perfect culmination of the Banks era. They scored 17 points (15 is a perfect team score in cross country). Nyambui, hobbled by an injury, was unable to defend his individual title, but was seventh overall and the fourth scorer on the team, earning his fourth All-American honor.

When I arrived in El Paso in fall 1983, the cross country team again won the national title after finishing fifth in new coach Heidebrecht's first year. I was sitting out the year as a redshirt because of my transfer status, but the ramifications were huge for me as well as others who were part of the program. Heidebrecht resigned a few months later, accused of handling a slush fund that funneled payments to his athletes and attempting to act as an agent for his world-class runners to endorse Diadora, an Italian racing-shoe manufacturer. Eventually, the 1983 title was vacated.

With so much uncertainty and bitterness in town, I wasn't sad to leave that summer for Atlanta, Georgia, where the Tanzanian runners, along with other international athletes, were training for the upcoming Los Angeles Olympics. My old coach, Ron Davis, had used his network in Africa and the US to set up a Pre-Olympic Training Camp with Andrew Young, Atlanta Mayor and former US Ambassador to the United Nations. The camp allowed young Olympic hopefuls as well as experienced Olympians, mostly from Africa, to use American facilities and have the opportunity to be seen by American coaches while preparing for the big event.

We were staying at Emory University, but I would travel to road races around the country, choosing longer events to prepare for the steeplechase again at the Olympics. I won the famed 10K Peachtree Road Race in Atlanta with a 28:35.0 and placed fourth at the Elby's 20K in Wheeling, Ohio, in 61:45. I also won a 10-miler in Bern, Switzerland, in 47:22.4. My conditioning was right where I wanted it to be, and I had improved my hurdling technique since the 1980 Games.

Unfortunately, so much road work took its toll. I developed shin splints and had to back off. By the time we were at the Olympic Village in UCLA just days before the Opening Ceremonies, I didn't know whether I'd be able to run. I kept testing my leg to see if I could run without pain. Each day, the answer remained no. Beyond the pain, I was concerned about doing lasting damage to my body if I attempted to run the three rounds of races needed to win the steeplechase. I had no choice but to bow out of my opening heat.

Julius Korir of Kenya took gold in 8:11.8—0.68 seconds faster than my silver-medal performance four years earlier. Joseph Mahmoud of France was second in 8:13.31, and Brian Demer of the US took bronze in 8:14.06. Could I have won at 31 years old? I can't say. I just knew that when I scratched, it was more than likely my last best chance at Olympic gold.

May 14, 1988, was a big day for me: the commencement ceremony where I received my bachelor's in education from UTEP.

//

School was nearly underway as the Olympic flame was extinguished. I returned to El Paso in a tough spot…injured, with a new coach, away from my pregnant wife and two children, and soon, without my scholarship. Because of sanctions against the university for Heidebrecht's slush fund, scholarships were cut for three years and the team was banned from competing at the national championships.

Making it to the 1988 Olympics in Seoul, South Korea, was still a wish of mine, but so was an education, which required money much sooner than that. The army allowed me to stay on leave, but I needed to pay most of my way. So, I decided to lose my amateur status. I never did run any cross country or track races as a UTEP Miner. My decision also meant that Seoul was out of the question.

In many ways, this was a great relief. I now had the opportunity to make money at road races and track meets around the world. It also meant that I had committed fully to getting my education degree as quickly as possible so I could return to my family and put it to use in my home country.

My wife and three children—Harriette was born in 1984—visited El Paso just a few times before I graduated in 1988 with a bachelor of science in education. Engelbert was Mama Bayi's helper with little girls to take care of. I would return home when I could, and we kept in touch as I traveled to races and kept up with my studies. I managed some solid performances over the next three years, and the Honolulu Marathon provided me some redemption at the 26.2-mile distance. I was 12th there (at 2:25:52) in 1985 and fourth in 1986 (2:16:22), the first time the race offered prize money. Kenya's Ibrahim Hussein won both years; behind him in '86 were three Tanzanians: Nyambui, Gidamis, and me.

Returning home to Tanzania in 1988 was in some ways very similar to when I returned home in 1980. This time, instead of being 27 years old, I was just about to turn 35. And instead of a medal in my bag I had a degree—but as before, I still had a lot of different directions that my life could go. I no longer had plenty of races in my future, but I felt sure I wasn't done yet either.

Training at UCLA just before I had to drop out of the 1984 Los Angeles Olympics because of shin splints.

After taking 1988 off, I concluded my competitive running career with two 1989 races in West Germany: the Bremen Marathon in April (15th place) and the 25K de Berlin on May 7 (26th place).

I felt that I had done my job in athletics. Now it was time to use my degree in service to my country and my family. I was proud that I had shown the fortitude in earning my degree just as I had done on the track. Even when I couldn't rely on my scholarship, I saw my goal and found a way to complete it. Of course, I couldn't have done it without Anna. She had supported me fully since the first day we met in 1974. Her sacrifice and strength was even greater than mine, as she had done the bulk of the work in raising our three beautiful children. I couldn't wait to become more involved with their day-to-day lives.

I returned to the army, this time primarily as a coach and sports administrator. Anna still handled the hair salon and poultry and prawns businesses and took care of matters in the home. We always felt good about these endeavors. Everybody needs food and wants to look nice. She had developed loyal customers. She and I never wanted to start something that didn't have a chance at success. You must have some idea who your clients will be. You start any service or product with an eye on who will use it.

We kept doing our jobs into the 1990s. I thought about where else I might be an administrator or educator after I retired from the service, but I didn't yet know when or where. Our children were now of school age. Like many Tanzanians who could afford it, we thought the schools in Uganda and Kenya were superior, so we sent them to Kenya. But we did so with mixed feelings. We missed them, of course, but we also felt like by sending money outside our borders, we weren't supporting our own country that we loved.

What we need is something for the community, we said. What we need might just be a school. Anna and I had always been practical people, and we didn't jump into action without a plan. We remained busy, as all young families are, but for the next few years that vision never completely left our minds.

CHAPTER 18

A Mighty Baobob Tree Starts as a Spinach

FOR HALF A DECADE OR MORE, WE CONSIDERED THE EDUCATIONAL opportunities for the youth in our country, and all the while we were saving as much money as we could to eventually, we hoped, build a school.

One question we asked ourselves was why we and other Tanzanian parents sent our children abroad. The simple answer was that we thought schools in Kenya and Uganda were superior. We were just doing what everybody else was doing. When we looked into it more and talked it over with friends, we decided the only reason for this assumption was that schools in those countries used English as the language of instruction.

Because English is the dominant language around the world, there was some logic in that assumption. It came at a cost though. We sent Annette and Harriette to a private school in Kenya, then to a government school, and then to a third school. Fees were high. Security was questionable. Occasionally, I needed to be in Nairobi on business. I would show up to the school unexpectedly, and if it wasn't visitation hours I had to wait to see them. Or I would have to talk to them from the other side of the fence. This did not feel right.

Even though, as in Tanzania, Swahili and English are both official languages in Kenya, the girls weren't speaking Swahili as often and they were losing their mother tongue. We didn't see them enough, and we feared they were losing the cultural values of our home country.

This would come through in big and small ways. When our daughters returned from Kenya for holiday, they would say in Kiswahili *nipe*, which sounds like a command ("give to me"), instead of saying *tafadhali naomba* ("please may I"). If you direct someone to "come here" in Kenyan Kiswahili, the words are *kuja hapa*. But in Tanzania, we add *tafadhali* ("please") and say *tafadhali njoo hapa*.

Those are subtle but important differences. Tanzania is a nation of *tafadhali*; we are a nation of "please."

We wondered what other cultural values and beliefs Tanzanian children were missing. We wanted our youth to be good citizens who believed in our nation and were prepared to contribute positively to society. After years of prayer and discussion, Anna and I got serious about what was possible in developing a school from scratch.

//

By 1991, I had been promoted to the rank of major in the air transport wing and still had many duties there in Dar es Salaam. Anna remained busy with so many jobs at home as a mother and as a businesswoman, even more so as our fourth child, a son we named Cuthbert, was born in 1992.

Still, in the evenings we would find time to discuss what we would do to create a school with instruction in Swahili that could achieve excellence. Our dream was starting to take shape. Together, we knew we had the skills necessary to be a success—from managing daily administrative tasks to handling a budget to developing and implementing a curriculum where students could achieve their best.

By 1996, we had a plan in place. We were using our own money, so we knew we had to start small. That was fine with us; the mighty baobob tree starts as a spinach.

At the start, we didn't even have money for classrooms—we used the garage in the house we built in the 1970s in Kimara, just outside Dar. We were committed to not taking out any loans for our venture. I didn't want to be put into a position where a bank or a person could take our school away.

It required patience and sacrifice to use our savings and grow slowly when we knew that many students could benefit from our school. Fortunately, life was relatively cheap in Tanzania at that time. We couldn't have moved forward if it was not. Mama Bayi, as our students quickly and affectionately came to refer to my wife, handled the day-to-day business of the school while I focused on discussing our philosophy with prospective parents and working with teachers on the curriculum.

Our money would be better spent on a quality instructor, we decided, and this was one of the most important early decisions we made. When we finally got the government permits and certifications approved for our first year, we hired a teacher from Kenya. Her name was Judith Ogoba Othiambo. This was a smart hire, not just because Judith was excellent at teaching young children, but because she was Kenyan.

As we started interviewing parents who were considering sending their children to our school—or rather, the parents were interviewing us!—inevitably one of the first questions would be where the teacher came from. Because Judith was from Kenya, parents had confidence that she was qualified. The parents heard the answer they wanted and proceeded to tell their friends. That response may sound silly when I say it now, but at the time, Tanzanians believed a Kenyan teacher was a better teacher. Anna and I had fallen into that same trap as parents. We saw the school as a small way to change our fellow citizens' view of our country. We wanted the people of our country to realize that English doesn't equal a good education; English is simply a means of communicating.

Over time, as the school gained more recognition, this became a non-issue, but I am grateful to this day that Judith, and our second hire, a Kenyan named Francis Kagotho, were both so good at their jobs and also came from our neighbor to the north.

Judith was in charge of Class 1—seven students ages four and five, who grew as the school did. In our second year, 1997–1998, those children moved to Class 2 in a room we constructed above the garage, while a new group of Class 1 students moved into the garage classroom. In total, we had 17 students. The sitting room and balcony of our house became additional classroom space and a dining room at snack and lunch times as we grew.

By year three, we had more than 30 students. Space was tight in Kimara, so we built up. Our one-story house was soon a full two-story house. We only spent what we made through tuition, my army salary, and Anna's income.

//

By 2003, our first class—kindergarten-age just seven years earlier—was now headed to secondary school. We had built bonds with those families, and we couldn't just hand them to another school. The families didn't want that, and neither did we. But space in Kimara didn't allow us to expand any more than we already had. We were surrounded on all sides: electrical high-tension lines on the south, a major road on the north, an escarpment to the east, and a river to the west. In addition, a secondary school would require sports facilities, which had always been a goal of mine anyway.

In Kimara, we had a small football pitch, about 40x20 meters. No way could we have regular teams and training in that limited space for our older student-athletes. Athletics for our elementary students up to that time had consisted of a single sports festival each year that was held at the University of Dar es Salaam or even the national stadium 20 kilometers (12.4 miles) away where I had run many successful races as a younger man.

The day we knew was coming had finally arrived. We needed to look for land where we could build a secondary school. With that would come the need for a loan. When we invested our own savings in the school back in 1996, we reminded ourselves: God is around. As we continued to add students into the hundreds, and every room of our ever-expanding house was filled with the sounds of learning and laughter, we felt blessed: God is still around. Even when money felt as tight as the classrooms, we didn't feel like we were struggling to make ends meet. Any money we received, we spent to accomplish our goals with the school: God is always around.

By 2000, we were taking a leap of faith that God would help guide us as we expanded to a new location. We were not worried. After searching for a property for several months, we found a 50-acre lot in Mkuza-Kibaha Area, 40 kilometers (25 miles) west on the major road out of Dar. It looked like it had tremendous potential for our school.

The lot at that time was surrounded by only a few houses. There was little commercial activity along the Dar es Salaam–Morogoro Road that far out, and we were three kilometers (almost two miles) farther off the highway. Mostly it was wide-open space. We took a chance that our families, many from Dar, would be willing to send their children this far away. The great thing was that it gave us lots of room to grow. Also, it was closer to rural families outside the city that lived in the interior of the country. We had always wanted to be accessible to students from all over Tanzania, and this spot might work to our advantage.

Once we found the Kibaha site, we got to work on the financing. We were fortunate to be eligible for a loan through the Tanzania Social Action Fund (TASAF), a new program created by the national government to use money received from the World Bank. This gave us more favorable terms than a traditional bank and ensured we would be able to help more students who needed assistance. We retained the autonomy to run our campuses efficiently and administer funds to students in need. The administration building, classrooms, kitchen, dining hall, and dormitories went up over three years, and in March 2005 Tanzanian President Benjamin William Mkapa officially opened the Filbert Bayi Secondary School.

Even better, the funding could be used to create a local health clinic, a tremendous benefit to the impoverished Kibaha community that surrounded our school site. Not only would local residents not have to find a way into Dar to get health care anymore and not only could our neighbors receive HIV/AIDS education and other health information close by, but also the creation of the clinic and the school provided more of our neighbors jobs in building and working at these sites.

One of many friendly encounters through the years with my inspiring African brother, Kip Keino.

As we sought a site for the new campus, we also created the Filbert Bayi Foundation to provide greater opportunities in physical activity and health for high-level athletes as well as the local community. I've always believed that sport leads to healthier individuals and can help them reach their full potential. We felt that the school's success gave us the ability to impact so many more people beyond the students in our care and their families. The foundation made that official. It has grown alongside the school for more than 20 years.

Starting a foundation was all new to me, but we believed it was an important part of fulfilling our mission. I was influenced greatly by my African brother Kip Keino and his commitment to serving his country after retiring from athletics. He and his wife, Phyllis, purchased a farm in Eldoret, Kenya, and converted it into an orphanage where they adopted dozens of children. Later, in 2000, they created the Kip Keino School. Anna and I were inspired by their sacrifice and dedication as we started our school in 1996 and rechristened it Filbert Bayi School.

//

Back when our Kimara campus opened in 1996, it did not have my name attached to it. The school was called St. Mary's. This made sense to me, as a nod to our Catholic faith. Our school provided religious instruction from the very beginning.

Beside the front door today, a plaque hangs as a reminder of the early days when we were still called St. Mary's. The plaque commemorates the start of construction of the main building that began when we had outgrown our garage and the second-floor addition of our small house: "The foundation stone for the St. Mary's Nursery & Primary School at Kimara was laid down by Hon. Prime Minister Frederic T. Sumaye on 23rd September 1998."

These are steps I've taken many times...the front entrance to our original campus.

The problem with the name "St. Mary's" is that there was another St. Mary's school in Dar at the time. That's not surprising. All over the world, there are many schools, hospitals, shelters, towns, and other entities named after Jesus's holy mother. She represents all that is good about motherly love—humility, mercy, commitment, sacrifice, and devotion—traits I've witnessed over a lifetime in my own mother.

In no way would I ever suggest that the name Filbert Bayi could or should compete with that of St. Mary. The problem was simply that people would think our St. Mary's School was connected to the other similarly named school in the area. We had to explain that we were independent. I don't know that we lost students because of this confusion, but it didn't help anybody for our identity to be unclear to potential families or the local community.

Parents were actually the ones who encouraged us to change the school's name. They convinced Anna and me that my name was well known throughout Tanzania. "Filbert Bayi," they told us, suggested excellence through an Olympic medal, two world records, and, when I retired as a major in 2001, 31 years of service to my country. Anna agreed immediately, and I knew better than to disagree with her.

We didn't have any Marys among our families. We did have my wife, and Saint Anne was Mary's mother, so I suggested that might be an option if we were to show truth in advertising. But our families, Anna, and I discussed it, and I believed using my name did make sense. Truly, I was honored and really liked the idea of my name being something that students aspired to emulate.

//

Ultimately, a school is defined as successful or not based on its results. That's not really so different than a race on the track, though the meaning of success, who defines it, and how results are measured are much cloudier in an educational environment.

We always felt that the culture we forged was key to making Filbert Bayi Schools something students and families would be proud to be

Classrooms like these at our elementary school are much more spacious than when we first opened in our garage in 1996.

associated with, whether on the front of an athletics jersey or at the top of a diploma. The emphasis on community has always been part of that culture. We set out to develop citizens who wanted to contribute to Tanzania's future, and we're still doing it today.

More than 1,200 nursery, primary, and secondary students now attend our two campuses each year from all over Tanzania and even outside the country.

"Sometimes I sit together with my wife and we can't believe this," I told CNN in 2014. "It's a miracle. Most of the students, they want to be professionals. They want to be IT people, they want to be pilots, doctors, be everything. We always tell them, if you want to be anything you have to work hard because those things won't come like a dream. You have to work hard, you have to commit yourself. Most teenagers don't think about the future, they think about now. So we always teach them, now will pass and then the future will come. And if you aren't prepared for the future you'll end up nowhere."

We have become a reliable partner for educational, health, and athletic organizations through the years, including hosting major events in our 1,500-capacity conference hall. In spring 2019, South Africa's esteemed ambassador, Thandi Lujabe-Rankoe, spoke to our students. She was a lion for justice in her own country and the African National Congress even before the apartheid era officially ended, and continued lobbying and leading aid projects for indigenous people, women's initiatives, and social investments all over the continent. During her stay she implored our students to work hard in their education and donated copies of her books, *Two Nations, One Dream and A Dream Fulfilled.*

My coach, Ron Davis (left), and I welcomed Ambassador Thandi Lujabe-Rankoe to the school in 2019.

//

As parents—I said it at the start of this chapter—Anna and I were just doing what everybody else was doing: sending our children abroad because we assumed they would be better educated there. As administrators, we strove to be different. We showed that in part by proving that teaching in Swahili could lead to a solid education and high-achieving students. Cuthbert got an opportunity his older siblings did not. He spent his entire primary and secondary-level years at Filbert Bayi Schools...and I assure you he didn't receive any favorable treatment!

Cuthbert gave us an opportunity as well. We got to watch him grow up right under our noses. I'm not one for regrets, but I do feel a little sad that we didn't have that opportunity with Engelbert, Annette, and Harriette.

Most parents I've ever met aren't sure they did a good enough job with their children. I can't say for sure whether we did or didn't. I can say Cuthbert finished his degree in business at a university in Malaysia and is back in Tanzania, married and a father. I just know that our parenting and professional lives came together with him at Filbert Bayi Schools...and I'm grateful for it. Those years felt right, and not all parents get that opportunity.

When I was confronting my greatest challenges on the track, I didn't know it then, but I was placing myself into the fire so I could be prepared for life's challenges and opportunities long after I was done racing. I was young and inexperienced in Munich, trying to figure out a new race and finding what worked for me in training and in competition. I was alone overseas in the US and Europe in 1974 and 1975, trying to figure out a new language and new racing formats, and again in the 1980s as I transitioned from racing to returning to school.

Through it all, I faced fears, adapted, and gained confidence when I overcame them, one at a time. I already *knew* the importance of sacrifice and commitment toward goals, but I experienced the truth of that only as I kept surpassing them.

In beginning Filbert Bayi Schools and the Filbert Bayi Foundation, I was just as inexperienced and committed to finding the identity that worked for me. Fortunately, I was not alone this time. Anna and I developed the school and foundation together, continuing the values that we had always lived individually and together to ensure we met our increasingly ambitious plans.

If you're just doing what everybody else is doing, well, that's about the same as running with the pack for three laps and then sprinting the final lap of the mile. That's the conventional way to do things, and it's not "wrong," exactly...but it's not the way to make a change in the world. Sometimes, you have to be different, be yourself, and see what happens. You might fail, but...you might succeed.

Athletics and the military gave me skills and opportunities that made it possible for me to give back to my country through our growing school and foundation. I still wasn't content to have just one job though. My career in athletics and administration combined to give me another means to serve Tanzania in leadership roles.

At work in my office in Kimara in June 2019.

CHAPTER 19

An Ambassador for My Sport and Country

I LOVE SEEING THE PAINTED ALPHABET ON AN EXTERIOR WALL IN Kimara—a is for apple, l is for lion, and so on. Or watching the big yellow bus with "Filbert Bayi Schools" written across the side departing to take children on a field trip.

In Kibaha, I drive on a bumpy road, past scooters and cars and a yellow street sign labeled "Br. YA Filbert Bayi" to get to the school. There, the tribute signs to Nelson Mandela and President Julius Nyerere welcome visitors at the entrance of campus. The indoor multisports complex sits directly in front, with the track surrounding the football pitch on the right.

Most importantly, the children walking around both sites create a constant, joyful energy.

From the first day of our campuses opening until now, I stay so busy and travel so often that sometimes I don't soak in all these sights and sounds. As I get older, I make a point to do so.

I'm not complaining. For more than two decades, Anna handled administrative matters onsite as the director, including overseeing what grew to become more than 100 employees. I have been chairman of the board, which means meeting with external partners, including donors, Ministry of Education officials, contractors, community leaders, and many more. It makes sense that I am often away.

I'm blessed to have a bustling nursery and elementary school in Kimara…

…as well as an active elementary and secondary school campus in Kibaha.

It has always been like this; it's almost like after many years of focusing on just running, I need to have multiple jobs and commitments to fill my days and find the next challenge to meet—challenges that often aren't as clear-cut as breaking the finish tape before seven other guys! I enjoy all that I do, so what would I give up anyway?

//

When I was still in the army in 2001, I was a senior officer, still required to be on active duty. I even missed the 2000 Olympics in Sydney, Australia, when I was a member of the technical committee of Tanzania National Athletics, because of military commitments. I had been given permission by military headquarters to be away as a national delegate in Sydney, but the paperwork hadn't come through.

My superior needed the permit from headquarters by the time we finished work at noon on a Friday. Our Olympic qualifiers were leaving on Monday. When the permit finally came at 9 a.m. on Monday, my post commander called me.

"Sir," I said. "The team has gone. It was a group ticket. I missed the flight."

The athletes and administrators could function in Australia without my presence, but needless to say it was a frustrating experience. As it turned out, I would have more opportunities to attend international sporting events in the new century—and many more opportunities to balance the demands of a school with national athletics administration.

Up to that point, I had been heavily involved with Tanzanian athletics for more than a decade since my retirement, by coaching promising runners in the armed forces and as a national coach for our distance runners at the 1992 Barcelona Olympics. We did not win any medals, but we performed well. I served as secretary of the national technical committee for five years, starting in 1992, and have continued as a member on it ever since. I also joined the technical committee of track and field's governing body, the IAAF (now called World Athletics), in 1999 and served for 16 years.

Since then, I have spent four years on the Commonwealth Games sports committee. For seven years, I was on the National Sports Council, including three on the technical committee and a term as the national course director in sports administration. I've taken and taught IAAF and Olympic Solidarity courses abroad in areas such as competition management, specialization coaching, and officiating, to ensure I stay up to date on the latest knowledge and best practices.

I've always enjoyed the minutiae of a technical committee's work. Essentially, we deal with making and adapting the rules. We do our best to provide the best competitive experiences for athletes and fans, and even though much of what we do goes unnoticed, it is important. We debate dozens of rules and procedures every time we meet. In a single session, we might cover anything from whether officials should measure a throwing event to the nearest centimeter or round down, to how much time an athlete should have to attempt their high jump or long jump, and whether to add an event to a meet.

These are the details that intrigue me. At heart, I'm a rule follower. I expect myself and others to have the discipline and commitment to play fair in whatever we do, and I also want the leaders of those endeavors to take seriously the responsibility to adjust those rules as necessary to ensure a level playing field, equity, and safety for all.

Notice that as a rule follower, I can still be creative in my approach to my work. In fact, sometimes being successful requires knowing the rules and thinking ahead of your competitors or whatever challenge is at hand. Just as I sought to determine how best to maximize my training and strategically race decades earlier, just as I methodically assessed how to prepare military aircraft for use, now I consider the effect of technology, the needs of meet officials, and the progression in talent of young athletes to make sure our events keep up with the times.

I was secretary general of Tanzania's National Olympic Committee from 2002 to 2012, and after stepping down was elected again in 2016. My current term will end after the 2024 Paris Games. It's a great honor to serve in that capacity. A lot of people are counting on me. Our successes and failures are a reflection of me, and because I'm competitive, I want to put my whole team in position to reach our goals. But there are many situations that are out of your control in an executive position like that. It requires diplomacy and patience to continue articulating the plan and pushing to meet our objectives. It's rewarding in a very different way than racing.

With all due respect to the high-level administrators out there, my duties on technical committees through the years gave me just as much pride. I receive a great deal of joy in seeing our behind-the-scenes work lead to exciting moments on the days where the athletes put their skills and training to the test on fields, courts, and tracks around the world.

//

Whatever position I've held and whatever work I've helped accomplish in these organizations, I've done my best to improve the competitive experience for the athletes. Particularly with the national jobs I've done, I have wanted more of my countrymen and women to represent Tanzania with grace and success on the global stage. We were building something strong in the 1980s, starting with the arrival of Ron Davis and Olympic medals won by Nyumbai and me, then continuing with performances by guys such as Zakariah Barie, Gidamis Shahanga, Agapius Masong, and Juma Ikangaa.

I want to recapture that, because I know how much talent and initiative there is in my country. The running culture in countries such as Kenya and Ethiopia is respected worldwide. We have that same potential, but we have not cultivated it consistently. I am committed to being part of the cultivation now so we can harvest a brighter sporting future.

It's not just about podiums, records, and international prestige, though there is great value in fielding world-class athletes that personify dignity and excellence for a country. It's also about inspiring your fellow citizens, giving back, and showing people who can relate to your upbringing and culture what they themselves might be capable of, if given the opportunity.

MILE WORLD RECORD HOLDERS AT 1994 COMMEMORATION

Fourteen of the world's 16 living mile-record holders convened at the Grosvenor House Hotel on May 4, 1994, then boarded a bus that took them to the Iffley Road track in Oxford, England, the site where on May 6, 1954, Roger Bannister ran the first recorded sub-4:00 mile in history. Standing, from left to right, are world record holders Arne Andersson (Sweden), John Landy (Australia), Herb Elliott (Australia), Michel Jazy (France), Filbert Bayi (Tanzania), John Walker (New Zealand), Steve Cram (United Kingdom), and Noureddine Morceli (Algeria). Seated are Roger Bannister (United Kingdom), Derek Ibbotson (United Kingdom), Peter Snell (New Zealand), and Jim Ryun (United States). Absent from this photo but attending the commemoration were Sebastian Coe and Sydney Wooderson, both of the United Kingdom. Absent from the commemoration festivities were Guilder Hägg (Sweden) and Steve Ovett (United Kingdom).

BACK TO THE FUTURE

//

Sometimes the quantitative and the qualitative align to show you what is possible.

Let me give you an example. On May 6, 1994, I joined 14 of the 16 living mile world record holders at the Iffley Road track in Oxford, United Kingdom. We were commemorating the 40th anniversary of the place where Roger Bannister broke the four-minute mile barrier. While the other members of our exclusive club wore sports coats, sweaters, or sweat suits, I proudly wore a blue and gold native robe Anna made for me.

I was the only sub-Saharan African in the bunch. Noureddine Morceli of Algeria, who had then held the mark of 3:44.39 for eight months, was the only one close to being as dark as me. I had been born 11 months before Bannister's feat. Oxford was so far removed from my mother's experience in the remote hills of Tanganyika that even if she hadn't been mourning my father, she wouldn't have known or cared about it. Yet, here I was, 40 years later, celebrating a footrace.

Like everyone else in attendance, I sought out autographs and reflected on the memories that brought me to my place in this strange human history, where people of all languages and backgrounds and political leanings care who can run four laps around a track the fastest.

"John, we've never done this before," I said to my closest friend there.

"This is a once-in-a-lifetime event, Filbert," replied John Walker.

"Yes, once in a lifetime," I said, looking back down at my paper to find out what signatures I was still missing (Smith, 1994).

There I was, at age 40, celebrating with Brits, Aussies, Kiwis, an American, a Swede, a Frenchman, and an Algerian, a continent away from my home, acting a little like a giddy schoolboy. If we were to hold the event today, there would be just 11 of us (the only additional invitee would be Hicham El Guerrouj of Morocco, whose 3:43.13 in 1999 eclipsed Morceli).

In that moment, though, I knew that I fully belonged with these other great men—who in addition to being very fast had gone on to become politicians, researchers, doctors, advocates, educators, administrators, and lords. And by extension, Tanzania belonged with those other great nations.

Trading autographs with the great Roger Bannister on a very special night in London, May 4, 1994.

"I don't have much money," I said at the event. "But I have this: I'm among the great milers in the world. That makes me rich" (Smith, 1994).

Running a world record mile has fascinated the world for more than a century, but never more so than when Bannister broke four minutes. Meeting with my brothers in Oxford, I recognized the humility and arrogance that comes with our individual feats. Gary Smith, the gifted *Sports Illustrated* writer who documented the 1994 Bannister commemoration, said we willingly "stepped into each other's shade" at that event. In some ways, we still do.

Over the years, I've often seen Sebastian Coe, now president of World Athletics, track and field's international governing body, at the Olympics, World Championships, and other major events. As chairman of the London Organising Committee in 2012, Lord Coe even visited Tanzania as a guest of the British Council, which organized a program called "Inspiration" to promote sport in various countries.

Sometimes, he will introduce me as "the guy whose world record I broke." To which I'll respond, "Yeah, but somebody broke your record too."

We smile, but we are also measuring the tension between the past, our responsibilities of the present, and what our futures hold.

Time is elusive. It eventually wipes away our numbers and humbles everyone, even those of us who at one time could say we did one thing better than anyone else ever had. We must make the most of the days we have. Even if we dwell on the past, as we did on May 6, 1994, and as I'm doing as I write this book, we shouldn't lose sight of the legacy we want to leave.

I firmly believe sport is a force for good. It's one of the few concepts on our planet that can bring love, harmony, and friendship to those who celebrate it, rather than intense division. I see the Olympic Movement as an opportunity to practice peace and understanding. The Olympic Truce, dating back to the ancient Games when the city-states of Greece would pause their wars during the Olympic festival, is a symbolic tribute to this ideal.

Tanzanian students take part in sports activities during Sebastian Coe's (far right) visit to Dar es Salaam in February 2012. I am watching, second from left.

//

Many years ago, I was quoted as saying the following: "To say that politics is not a part of sports is not being realistic. When I run, I am more than a runner. I am a diplomat, an ambassador for my country."

People have misconstrued this to focus on the first sentence. They say I desire for geopolitics and sports to be entwined. In fact, I do not. All four Olympics I trained for were saddled with political interference—either terrorism or boycotts. Some affected me directly and others did not, but I would have personally preferred the three boycotts didn't occur. Even when I wholeheartedly agreed with the rationale behind the African countries' refusal to participate in 1976 and was fully willing to give up my opportunity to compete, I would have preferred all athletes get their chance. Yet when the cause is just, I do believe sports should step aside to do what is right.

What I meant by this statement was something else entirely. That's what I meant by the second sentence. I see sport as an opportunity for leaders of all kinds to be a different kind of representative, a person who fosters healthy competition and goodwill while showcasing the best of their country. That's what I've committed to in my lifetime of service to my sport, my country, and the Olympic Movement. I will continue this until I'm gone, knowing that sometimes what we do is not recognized until we're no longer alive, if even then.

I must admit that at times I feel my accomplishments are forgotten. I am not in the World Athletics Hall of Fame, which was established in 2012. It requires at least two Olympic or World Championship gold medals plus at least one world record, but it also allows for "athletes whose achievements had an extraordinary impact on our sport to be considered as well."

At the mile celebration in 1994, while holding onto my baby boy Cuthbert and a glass of water, I made a comment to Gary Smith that appeared in *Sports Illustrated*. Smith said I "watched with wonder and a little sadness. 'Other countries honor their history so much more than mine does,' Bayi said. 'In Tanzania I am no one. Maybe one day people will understand. That will be maybe when I die.'"

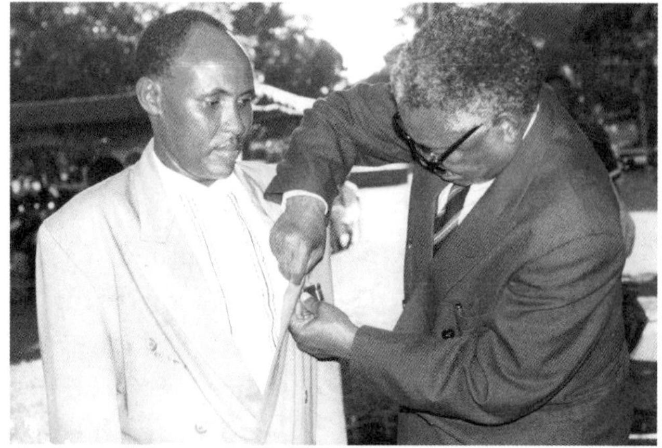

Receiving Tanzania's Medal of the Union from President Ali Hassan Mwinyi (upper left photo) and greeting Zanzibar President Ali Mohamed Shein.

Perhaps I sound like an aggrieved, embittered old man when I speak of oversights, and I don't intend that. I very much appreciate politicians and leaders who mention us golden oldies at gatherings many years after we competed. Old is gold…not trash.

Truly, I've lived a blessed life. Running has given me a chance to meet people and go to places I never could have dreamed of as a boy. But I do want to be recognized. When I see countries and organizations recognize their sporting heroes, it inspires others to be their best. Everyone benefits when people are at their best.

I've had many wonderful experiences and celebrations. In my own country, I was honored with the prestigious Medal of the Union by Ali Hassan Mwinyi. He was Tanzania's second president, after Julius Nyerere in 1985 became the first African head of state to voluntarily step down. On the continent, I was elected to the Africa Athletic Hall of Fame in 2012. I received the Commonwealth Games Sports Administrator of the Year Award in 2006 and a special lifetime achievement award from the Commonwealth Games General Assembly in 2018.

Sometimes, I realize that honoring another's achievements can be more powerful than celebrating your own. After all, people in other countries inspire their fans to be their best, too.

Two of the most meaningful events I ever attended were in New Zealand to celebrate my dear friend John Walker. After his book, *John Walker, Champion: An Autobiography* was released in 1984, they flew me from El Paso to Auckland, New Zealand, to surprise him. He was still competing strong—the next year he became the first man to run 100 sub-4:00 miles—but it was a "This is your life, John Walker" type of atmosphere. He didn't know I was there until they announced my name and I walked into the room.

In 1996, Walker announced that he had been diagnosed with Parkinson's disease. He and his wife, Helen, held an event to raise money for Parkinson's research. Anna and I joined other great runners and their wives to travel to Auckland to support the cause. I auctioned off a replica of the singlet I wore in Christchurch for the world record, and we had a relaxing evening of fish and chips at the Walkers' house the following night.

He and I remain lifelong friends, decades past our competitive days. It will always be one of my greatest honors to be connected in people's minds to John Walker.

//

Sometimes, my connection with Walker and other runners appears in unexpected ways. Dariusz Janczewski released an electronic music album

Dariusz Janczewski's illustrations, including one of me, for the liner notes of his album, *Milers*.

called *Milers* in 2010, with songs called "Filbert Bayi," "John Walker," "Steve Ovett," "Roger Bannister," "Derek Ibbotson," and "Peter Snell."

Janczewski, who now lives in the United States, ran for Poland before defecting in 1984. He was a sub-4:00 miler and a 1500-meter runner and steeplechaser, just like me. He even remembered warming up for the 1500m at the same time I was preparing for the 800m at a 1977 meet in Bydgoszcz, Poland—"while participating in track and field in those years, it was impossible for anyone to be unfamiliar with Mr. Bayi," he remembered.

He is a graphic designer by trade, and also an artist, photographer, and writer—the album was simply a labor of love from an amateur musician, Janczewski said. Here's his statement when asked why he included a song about me:

> Mr. Filbert Bayi, like the other stars of the middle-distance running that I included on my music CD, was one of the world record holders. He was a legend and a very versatile runner. He was able to compete, on the world level, in both middle distances and in steeplechase races—a quite rare combination. The secondary reason had to do with seeing him in person, as well as his history of racing in the Moscow Olympics

> against Bronisław Malinowski, the Polish steeplechaser I also raced with on a few occasions but never really knew in person.
>
> The music track "Filbert Bayi" on *Milers* is minimalistic in style. It has a cadence of patience and persistence of a distance runner. The pace of the tune resembles a quiet and graceful running style of many African athletes, like Filbert Bayi, Kipchoge Keino, Henry Rono, or Abebe Bikila. It seems effortless but it is economical, purposeful, and highly effective. In the music track, I wanted to convey all these qualities in slow-motion, like we see in a film. But there is also the mystery of Bayi. The Tanzanian runner's piercing eyes, his slim and almost modest statue, to me, epitomized those African distance runners who showed the world that fast, world-class running is about more than fame and financial gain, that running is a noble lifestyle.
>
> The words "top of the world," which appear in the song, are not there to glorify a victory of one runner over another. The words are there to remind us that running is one of the most beautiful of all human capabilities. This philosophy is in large part due to my witnessing the African athletes, such as Mr. Filbert Bayi, do what they have done so beautifully for so many years: run.

So yes, in a variety of important and surprising ways, I am remembered—as are men I raced against and admired. When I heard Janczewski's song and saw his professional work, I asked him to be the graphic designer for my book.

The connections we runners forge are mysterious and forever.

//

A dream of mine is to become a member of the International Olympic Committee. As stated in the Olympic Charter, "Members of the IOC represent and promote the interests of the IOC and of the Olympic Movement in their countries and in the organisations of the Olympic Movement in which they serve."

IOC members are voted on by existing members. I know how hard I would work there. I have always promoted the Olympic values as an athlete and administrator. Whether I'm ever officially chosen or not, that will not change.

I'm nearly 70 years old now, and, like everyone, I've become more acquainted with death and have seen up close the lure of memory and the limits of mortality.

Nowhere did that dark reality appear larger to me than January 6, 2021.

Receiving the Olympic flame from Charles Nyange (right) as the torch for the 2008 Games made its way through Dar es Salaam.

CHAPTER 20

Mama Bayi

My wife and I, along with our daughter Harriette and her husband and two young daughters, took a family road trip in late December 2020. We visited my mother in Karatu and other relatives there.

It was a relaxing visit after a hectic semester. Our schools had been closed for three months when the COVID-19 pandemic took the world by surprise in early 2020. Tanzania and most of Africa was fortunately spared the worst of it. In the fall we worked hard to create some sense of normalcy again.

On Christmas Day, while I stayed behind in Karatu, Anna and the others drove to her hometown of Moshi to visit relatives she had there and her mother's gravesite. Then they began the long drive back home to Dar es Salaam for a work commitment on December 27.

After that evening's event, Anna said she wasn't feeling well and they took her to the hospital. Her condition stabilized and was told she could rest at home in Kibaha. I arrived the next day, but she took a turn for the worse and an ambulance took her to the intensive care unit at Shree Hindu Mandal Hospital in Dar.

Over the next week, she did not improve, and I was feeling ill as well. Doctors said perhaps I was in shock or dealing with stress, but I came to see her as often as I could. Harriette told me she could see the fear in my eyes as I looked at Anna through the glass window in her hospital room. It was clear she was in trouble.

Around 8 p.m. on January 6, 2021, the doctor said what we all could see was coming. "We've done everything we could," he said.

Our final trip to Arusha and Moshi together had been so much fun, but looking back none of us realized how much pain she was going through. It was as though she fought long enough to say goodbye to her family.

With my mom, Magdalena (center), and wife, Anna (right). It was the last photo we took with these two beautiful women together, in Karatu, December 2020.

I may feel forgotten at times, but I assure you that I can never say enough about my wife, Anna. She worked with passion, conviction, confidence—and most of all with love for everyone she encountered.

Much of the time, she took care of the details so I could continue other responsibilities. This included allowing me to train so I could gain glory as a runner, or taking care of accounting, managing staff, and all the challenges that arise every day while I continued my careers in the army and sport. We made a great team, but she truly made it all work—our parenting, our school, our foundation, our finances…our lives. We built so much together and wanted to do more. Simply put, from the time I met her at the University of Dar es Salaam sports fields almost 50 years ago, she was my reason for being.

These days, she still is.

//

We were married more than 43 years. It had never dawned on me that she'd leave this earth before me. I still haven't come to terms with it, but those first few weeks I was in a daze, physically and mentally exhausted. The Saturday after she passed, we held a requiem mass and buried her at our Mkuza residence in Kibaha, beside the school. I received heartfelt condolences from around the world, including from former competitors and their wives. Anna was well known in her own right in Tanzania and across Africa.

Anna and I enjoyed taking photos together.

Newspaper articles focused intently on her interest in netball, and it was appropriate to do so. The *Tanzania Daily News* wrote: "Anna Bayi—Netball legend laid to rest." She was a good netball player when she was young, and she'd been determined to give back to the sport. Anna served as chair of the Tanzania Amateur Netball Association (Chaneta) from 2009 to 2013 and contributed greatly to the sport in our country. Most visibly, during her tenure as Chaneta chair, the national team made its first appearance in the International Netball Federation rankings, reaching fourteenth in the world and third in Africa.

Anna and I receive a customized shirt and ball from a World Teqball Federation official when we launched the emerging sport as part of the OlympAfrica Center at our Kibaha campus. OlympAfrica is an Olympic Solidarity program administered through national Olympic committees to promote community sport. Our Foundation has an office and we hold regular events on campus.

But that only happened because of the work she did behind the scenes for many years—on top of all her other home and work responsibilities—to seek funding for the sport and prioritize it at a grassroots level. The sport was only minimally popular for many years in Tanzania, so she would find athletic girls who didn't know the sport and made sure they learned the fundamentals. She prioritized Zanzibar and the mainland cooperating to identify and develop players. She awarded scholarships to talented students in many sports at Filbert Bayi Schools, but especially netball and athletics.

Tanzania hosted international netball competitions, including the African Netball Cup Tournament for the first time, which provided exposure to the sport for many girls. For many years, our school team was one of the country's best, including national champions twice.

//

In or out of sports, my wife's indomitable spirit always shined. She showed love and support to everybody she encountered.

After she was gone, there was so much to do—so much that she normally did—and I had no strength for it. My children and the committed staff and faculty, also saddened at her loss, got me through this period. I was able to remember her in private and get healthy again. We observed a 40-day mourning period, then held a memorial at which hundreds of people came through to pay their respects, from government officials and leaders of many sports governing bodies to relatives, friends, students, and parents of our school family. Shirts were made for the occasion with these words surrounding her picture: "Mrs. Anna Filbert Bayi, 1957–2021, Forever In Our Hearts."

Everybody had a memory about my Anna and I took them all in. She was such a driven person, able to be a disciplinarian as easily as she could provide a loving touch, whether to students, employees, or her family. Elizabeth Mjema, assistant managing director at the school, remembered how she once got a call at home from Anna one evening. Elizabeth had left the office air conditioner on at the Kimara campus, and Anna said she needed to return to the office and switch it off. You can bet that the AC was never left on again!

But she also recalled how Mama Bayi would spend time under the mango tree telling stories and emphasizing education with students while listening to what they had on their minds. Anna consistently encouraged all staff and students to take pride in the school grounds, present themselves professionally, and develop new skills and hobbies.

Elizabeth was touched when she recalled Anna's response to the death of Elizabeth's mother. "We were arranging for the burial of our beloved mum," Elizabeth said. "She came to our house holding a basket of food with a very special meal for me. She couldn't have known that I hadn't had anything since the day before. She took me aside while holding my hands and talked to me with words of comfort and love and care. She took care of me just how my mum did when I was hurt. At that moment, I felt like I needed someone to take on the loss of my mother and she was the one."

Our nephew Abdulnasser Fadhili Walele had been the ring bearer at our wedding when he was a small boy, but as a grown man he presented a moving eulogy for Mama Bayi's funeral service. He talked about when she and Baba Bayi (me!) took our children and the cousins to the Mororogo national parks or Bahari Beach for family picnics, and when he was able to get devoted time to talk with his aunt without many other children around.

From left: Harriette, Anna, and Elizabeth Mjema, who has worked at Filbert Bayi Schools and Foundation for more than 20 years.

Here is a portion of his speech:

> Mama, those countless hours of conversations were one of the best gifts you gave me. Thank you so much for all the things that you taught me. Mama, one of the best things about you is that you did not only teach us by words, but you actually demonstrated everything by actions. Mama, you are leaving us with many great gifts but I would like to mention just a few:
>
> **Hardworking:** Mama, you are the best definition of a hardworking person. What you have done for our entire family speaks for itself and everyone can clearly see that. Mama, your determination and focus paid off and we can all see for ourselves what an amazing work you and Baba Bayi were able to accomplish together. What a great team.
>
> **Love:** Thank you for the gift of love that you gave to all of us children, to our entire family and all of those who were fortunate enough to be in your circle of life.
>
> **Faith:** Mama, you always demonstrated your dedication and true commitment to our Heavenly Father. Thank you for sharing the knowledge and teachings of the Gospel and our Lord and Savior Jesus Christ.
>
> **True Love:** Mama, we thank you for demonstrating to all of us children what true love is. Your love to Baba Bayi and Baba Bayi's love to you is the best example for all of us children to take and to hold.

That last one really hits home. I completely agree with Abdul. I have been blessed with a loving family…

Our loving family continues to grow. I have 11 grandchildren—including two born in the past year since Anna passed—and one great grandson. Our youngest son got married in summer 2022, so I now have another daughter-in-law. We remember each and every day what a force Anna was: tough, strict, hardworking, and always putting others' needs above her own.

Harriette started working at our schools when she was back home for the holidays during college. She'd keep herself busy in the office, learning how things ran. After earning her business management degree in 2013, she became a full-time administrator. Mama and I always told her we sent her to college to assist us at our schools. She does just that and has made us proud.

"Mama was a kindhearted woman," Harriette said. "I did not always understand why Mama was so hard on me, but I now understand that my parents made sure I could lead and be better."

Harriette asked her oldest daughter what she remembered about Mama Bayi. "She told me always to pray," 5-year-old Elsa said. Harriette had her third child, a baby boy, in February 2022. "In those final weeks,"

Sharing a laugh with daughter Harriette and Mama during a send-off ceremony for Harriette. As part of the celebration, she gave her parents gifts.

Taking care of grandfather duties at Elsa's baptism.

she said, "all I could think about was how can I do this alone? With my other two children, you were here, Mama! But she taught me to stand on my own and that I would be fine.

"Mama will always be pure love, not only to me but to my family, siblings, and the society she lived in. My years being raised by her and dad have been nothing but the best memories. My two daughters are blessed to have known their grandmama and they will love her forever. I have dedicated my life to continue working with Filbert Bayi Schools, a legacy my parents created."

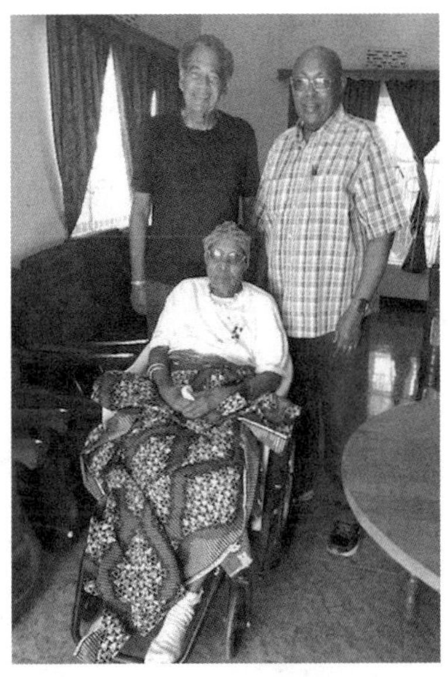

With my coach and brother, Ron Davis, and my mom.

The legacy continues in unexpected ways. Judith and Francis, the Kenyans who were the first teachers we hired, stayed at the school many years and later got married. To me, they are a symbol of how the school Anna and I started continues to foster love and connection beyond just the two of us. Mama Bayi's caring heart lives on not just in our family but in so many others who have gone through our school for more than 25 years.

When I say confidence, sacrifice, and commitment are the keys to success, I'm not just referring to building a racing career or a school; I'm talking about building a partnership and a family. All of that was always more meaningful and easier with Anna. The year 2021 was the hardest of my life because for the first time since I was 20 years old, I had to face it without her. I could handle loneliness on the road in countries whose languages I didn't understand, malaria, injuries, uncertainty about how to pay for school, and anything that came my way because I knew Anna was waiting for me in Tanzania—well, not waiting, exactly. She was managing businesses and our kids and making sure everybody stayed in line. She didn't have time to passively sit and wait for me. But I knew she was thinking of me as much as I was thinking of her. I loved her dearly. She was my rock. Now, I know she is still waiting for me in the same way in heaven. I'm sure she's keeping lots of angels very busy.

Family portrait with (from left) Engelbert, Cuthbert, Anna, Harriette, me, and Annette.

At the end of Harriette's send-off, Anna and I had the chance to say nice things about our daughter.

CHAPTER 21

A Tartan Track Before I Die

MY ANNA IS ON MY MIND EVERY DAY SINCE SHE PASSED, AND I SUSPECT she will be until I join her. That is comforting. I take on my daily tasks and responsibilities with vigor, in part because I know her spirit will always be with me.

The rhythms of the school year and the Olympic and Commonwealth quadrennials provide a measure of consistency for the work I do. Unfortunately, some things never change—as I was finishing the writing of this book, a bout of malaria slowed me down for several days. Still, many changes, big and small, sad and joyful, swirl around me. Examples are everywhere:

- My grandchildren and great-grandson keep me active as they grow up so fast. Our daughters and their families live close by, so the kids run around the school grounds and the house when they stop by to visit.
- Three of my siblings have died, including two in the past five years. Another lives in Dar es Salaam, one up north in Tanga, and three more still live in Karatu District in Arusha Region. I see them when I'm back home to visit my mother—speaking of a measure of consistency!
- Shortly after my wife died, her sister—a longtime matron at the school—also passed away.

- In March 2021, Tanzanian President John Magufuli died in office after an illness and Samia Suluhu Hassan took over the rest of his term.
- My running brother and great friend Suleiman Nyambui is back in Dar after coaching in Brunei. Instead of doing punishing workouts together, we now see each other regularly when he visits my school to provide tips for our young runners. One thing we still do is laugh loud and long when we are together. "He's not my friend or teammate or training partner," Nyambui said once. "Bayi is my brother and my family."

My youngest son, Cuthbert, says I am a simple man, and I suppose that's true. I do the work that needs to be done each day, as Secretary General of the National Olympic Committee until my term expires in 2024 and at the school for much longer than that. That is living, to me. Mama Bayi knew so much. When she was at the school, things got done. People responded favorably to her. She was clear, kind, and consistent in her expectations and how she treated people. She handled so many responsibilities at the school, clinic, and foundation, and made sure others took care of theirs.

I know I don't have forever, so I keep busy while I can to make the most of living. I've been fortunate enough to be on the earth nearly 70 years. I've seen the birth of my country, the death of apartheid, the evolution of my sport, and most important of all, the growth of my family and thousands of students who have come through my school.

Running made much of that possible for me. Events like the World Athletics Heritage Mile Night in Monaco just months before the COVID-19 pandemic hit provide reminders of a long-ago past that I will always cherish. For many, those memories are now filtered through YouTube clips and scattered Internet photos. But those of us in attendance to celebrate the mile that evening had *lived* them.

There I saw seven of the men I chased autographs with in Oxford back in 1994. Sadly, the great Peter Snell suffered a heart attack just before his flight to Monaco and was unable to come. He died three weeks later at age 80. My good friend John Walker was there. Largely silenced by Parkinson's disease, he remains a commanding presence in every room he's in with lively eyes that speak for him. Knighted in 2009, serving several terms in Auckland government, and raising horses with his wife, Helen, he has lived a full life.

The Heritage Mile Night put on by World Athletics in 2019 was a special celebration...

Forty-five years later, still sharing the stage with my good friend John Walker.

"It is true that Filbert and I are somehow connected with a very special bond," Walker wrote recently to a friend. "It is hard to explain but I think we were somehow meant to be a part of each other's lives. We have the greatest respect and love for each other and, yes, very different from my friendships with other competitors. I feel we are very similar in that we have the same outlook on life and we want to help others to succeed and live a happy life. We do not really discuss our legacies when we get together. We talk about our families and our dreams. We do not look backwards."

This photo includes people who were mile world record holders and/or 1500m World champions and/or Olympic champions, or their family representatives if the runner was deceased. Front row, left to right: Ron Delany, Michel Jazy, Erin Bannister, Jim Ryun, Lindsey Armstrong (Leather), me, Gabriella Dorio, Paola Pigni, John Walker, Charlotte Bannister, Steve Cram, Noureddine Morceli, Abdi Bile, Hicham El Guerrouj, Kipchoge Keino, Eamonn Coghlan, and Sebastian Coe.

Hicham El Guerrouj, the latest member of the mile world record club—holding it for two decades and counting now—was there as well. If the rest of us represented the past, he is the present. Who is our future?

Also there was my African brother Kip Keino. And Eamonn Coghlan, the fierce Irish competitor who caught me in Kingston and helped push me to a final lap that earned me the mile world record, which in turn secured the invite on this day, 44½ years later.

Enjoying a chat with my friend, Lord Coe.

So much has changed since I started racing. It is now entirely normal for pacesetters to take home more money for three laps worth of work than I did as an amateur over more than a decade of podium finishes and two world records.

And just the men, from left to right: Michel Jazy, Jim Ryun, me, Sebastian Coe, John Walker, Steve Cram, Noureddine Morceli, and Hicham El Guerrouj.

Brett Davies addressed this on the Runner's Tribe website in January 2022, on Walker's 70th birthday:

> "Prior to the spectacular successes of Coe, Ovett, Cram and Moroccan Said Aouita in the 1980s, it was due to athletes like Walker, Bayi and Coghlan, that the mile was such a popular event in the '70s. The athletes of today owe an enormous debt to athletes like Walker, who struggled against the strict amateur codes which still existed in the '70s, which prevented athletes earning a living from the sport, despite bringing big crowds and widespread television coverage to events…By the early-80s, sponsors began to invest big money in the sport. With the aid of promoters…athletics became hugely popular and athletes began to receive lucrative shoe sponsorships and cash prize money…with the advent of the European Grand Prix series."

Occasionally, I am pleasantly surprised to hear stories about the impact I had on others. Walker's longtime training partner and great friend, Rod Dixon, said that Bronisław Malinowski was well aware of me in the mid-'70s, long before he edged me to win Olympic gold in Moscow. "Bruno" trained with them in New Zealand when I broke my world records. My racing style prompted him back then to run shorter races to gain speed, Dixon said, and Bruno knew that I could be a threat in the steeplechase in 1980—maybe even before I did.

Dixon, who took fourth in my Christchurch world record race before moving on to longer distances and eventually winning the 1983 New York City Marathon, expressed gratitude for the impact I had on him and Walker. Walker and I were friendly when we competed, but we were still rivals and leery of sharing too much. Dixon has no such problem:

> When I went to road races and set my goal for New York City, I still did my track training based on the mile. I always saw myself as a miler, even as a marathoner. My heart and soul were there. When Filbert Bayi came along, I thanked him and honored him for redefining how it should be run, without all these rabbits and setups, running three laps quietly and then sprinting. He woke us up to how it should be run. You couldn't count on it always being run a certain way. The mile became more popular and successful again. Then John Walker was the first under 3:50 and redefined the whole attitude. I know John developed his attitude and focus based on that race with Filbert.

Sharing a relaxing moment in Monaco with Mama Bayi (center) and Kip Keino (right).

Dixon has developed his KiDSMARATHON program that promotes exercise and nutrition education to young children. He talks passionately about running and downplays the emphasis on winning. Interestingly, he says I help inspire that message:

> Our champion is the tortoise. Slow and steady wins the race. I go into schools and kids have that mentality that if you're not first, second, or third, you're a loser. I show that video from '74 and tell them to run your own race. Look at this man! He ran his own race. You do your own thing. You don't have to win the race to be who you are. That race that Filbert won has had a huge influence in everything I do. The Commonwealth Games was one of my defining movements. And that's Filbert. He's part of my life and my journey.

//

With so many memories and so much change, most of the time I focus intently on the future—even if sometimes that has me looking to the past. In 2018, I brought back my coach, Ron Davis, to provide a spark for our schools' runners as he did me.

> Ron Davis is my friend and my coach, and he's my brother. I invited him because I wanted him to come back to Tanzania and see what we are doing. Ron taught me that if you want to do something, you have to have a vision and you have to have a mission. And I think what he was teaching me when I was running is what I am doing now. For him, I think Tanzania is like his home. For me to invite him back is like inviting my brother to be back home and be with us. (Schrag, 2019)

For the next 3 ½ years, Davis remained the consummate coach, as dedicated as he ever was. He confidently prepared training plans for them, then pushed them, listened to them, and cared about them. The two of us at work were never just athlete and mentor, administrator and coach, Tanzanian and American. We were a team. We spoke regularly these past few years about our early sessions together in 1979-80, about the glory days with Nyambui, Barie, Shahanga, Masong, and Ikangaa, and others who had brief international success years later…John Yuda, Samson Ramadhani, and Christopher Isengwe. More recently, Alphonce Simbu and a woman, Failuna Abdi Matanga, are showing promise by qualifying for World Championships, Olympics, and other high-level competitions.

With those names as motivation, we mostly talked about how to nourish the talented athletes we have to develop enduring success. The future of athletics in Tanzania is happening before our eyes at Filbert Bayi Schools, we said. We strive to educate the finest students and athletes in the country, no matter where they may live or what their financial situation is. It is a way to give back to our country, including helping our promising students earn scholarships to study and compete in the United States through a program called "2020 and Beyond."

Back when Davis was hired as the national coach, much more funding from the federal government was available to train the best. There was a concerted effort to engage the ports authority, national utilities, the police, the prison service, and the military to recruit athletes, much like in Kenya and other African countries.

Now, schools and other organizations must make that investment without a sponsor and with facilities that are the best we can do. At the national championship meet in 2020, we had many young athletes perform exceptionally. Filbert Bayi Schools won the national title even though we were often competing against older athletes.

Our mission has not changed, but sadly, my brother, Ron Davis, died on April 22, 2022, after a short stay in the hospital at age 81. He brought glory to Tanzania in training me and stated clearly many times to me that he would be happy to die in his adopted country. In accordance with his wishes, his children agreed to have him buried at my family compound. For a man who made friends with seemingly everybody he met, it was one last act of connection, joining the Bayi and Davis families forever.

Meeting with former Tanzanian Minister of Information, Culture, Arts, and Sports, Harrison Mwakyembe (center), and Ron Davis (right) at Benjamin Mkapa Stadium shortly after Davis returned to the country in 2018.

I'm forever grateful for the work Davis did in establishing our "2020 and Beyond" program. Our first runner to earn that opportunity came in late 2021. Regina Mpigachai, a two-time Tanzanian national champion in both the 800m and 1500m, was supposed to start at the University of Northern Colorado a year earlier, but the pandemic delayed her collegiate career. "We are really making good development and it is always nice to see the mission you set as a school accomplished," I said in the announcement after Regina arrived in the US. "We're looking forward for more because our aim is to produce top-class athletes embedded with a quality education background."

Her new coach at UNC, Wayne Angel, said it well in his Facebook post:

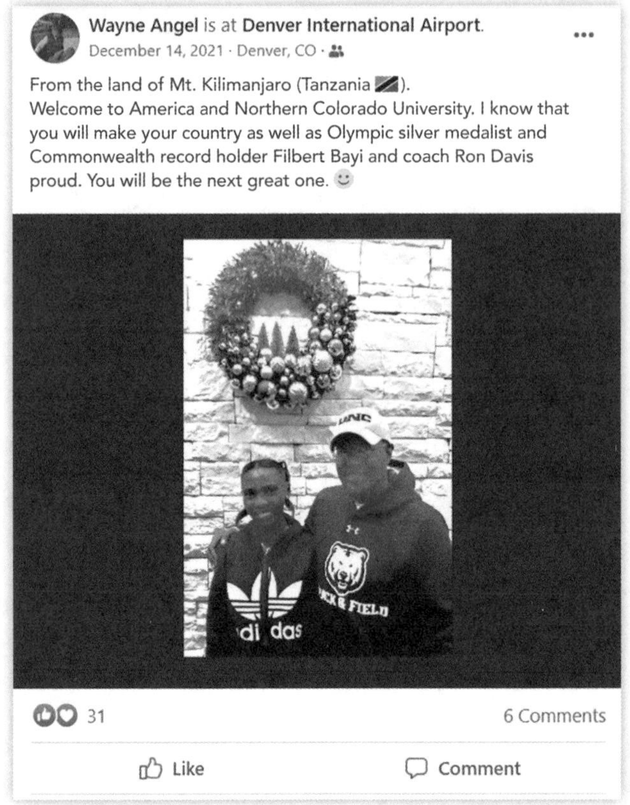

Immediately, Regina made an impact at UNC. She won her first three races at three different distances, and smashed the school indoor record in the 3000m.

The next generations keep coming. My grandkids will become adults and find their way, I hope with confidence, commitment, and sacrifice. Regina will strive to get a degree abroad as I did, and to do great things in the world. I anticipate she will be the first of many who trained under Davis to do so.

Life continues to roll on…with God and Mama Bayi and Coach Ron Davis looking down on me every day.

//

I have a dream that has occupied my mind for years now. In this case, it is a legacy not of people but of presence…it has eluded me, but I'm still chasing it.

I want a modern track at the Kibaha campus. Thousands of runners could pursue their dreams there. Coaches can craft workouts more effectively. Fans can watch high-level competition. Local residents can use the facility for exercise. I chased buses as a young man, but I would have loved to have the chance to run regularly on a smooth surface.

There are only three rubberized-surface tracks in all of Tanzania: one on the island of Zanzibar, one on the island of Pemba, and one at Benjamin Mkapa Stadium in Dar. This sounds like a simple request—in European and American cities, you can find these every few blocks, it seems. However, it is not a simple process. Nor is it cheap. I know, because I have sought funds for years. We have put proposals out to potential partners in recent years for a stadium on campus that would include not just a track but other features that would make it the best sea-level training center in East Africa. It would have bleachers for up to 5,000 people, an artificial turf football pitch on the infield, space for top-notch field events to be held, a wellness and fitness center, and an expansion of the community health clinic.

The goal is to enhance sporting opportunities at the competitive as well as community levels. It is an extension of Anna's and my belief for pretty much our whole adult lives that sport is an ideal means to better develop communities and individuals.

The Filbert Bayi Foundation has stepped forward in recent years to host national and regional championships in table tennis, volleyball, and judo. The 2015 Tanzanian National Athletics Championships were held at our dirt track facility. In some cases, these events had ceased to exist for several years because of lack of funds—this is unacceptable if Tanzania is to regain its place of prominence on the international sport stage.

I envision everything from secondary school championships and all-comers meets to training camps and clinics to international events

We have developed the Filbert Bayi Schools campus in Kibaha to be a wonderful site for school and sports, including a track and indoor multipurpose facility (far left of the photo).

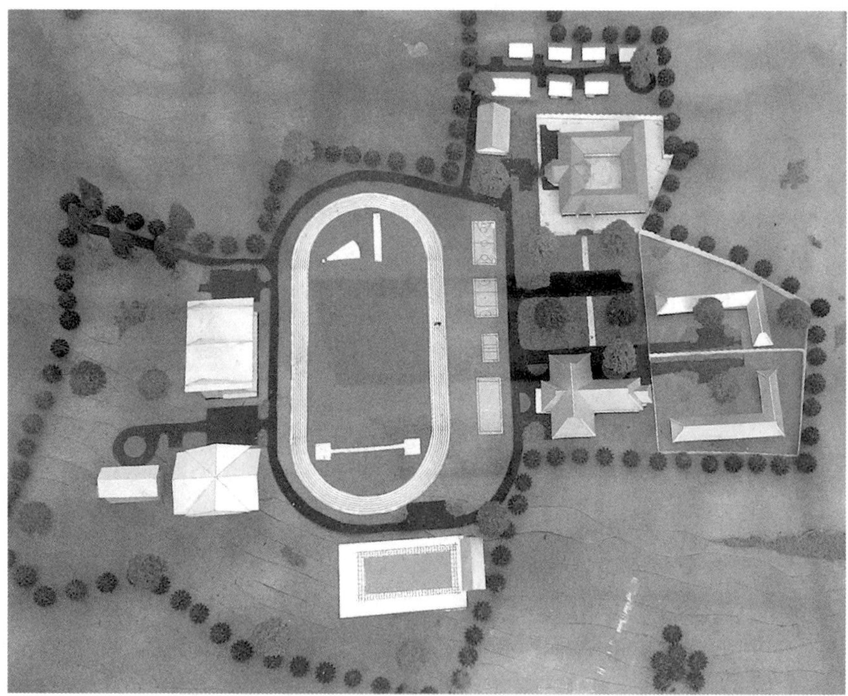

Our vision for the future sports complex includes a Tartan track and a swimming pool.

and training partnerships being possible if we can, step by step, reach this goal. A steady dose of commitment, sacrifice, and confidence is needed to get there, as with anything big you aspire to achieve.

Here is what I wrote in one proposal, explaining my personal conviction for wanting the track:

"For many years, I had this dream of creating an institution that would create an environment whereby the existing abundant sports talents can be developed to its full potential. This dream came about after witnessing painful experience where young sports talents had been wasted due to lack of simple but crucial resources and inadequate patronage to hopeful young ones...

"My strong conviction is that participation in sports naturally leads to healthy individuals at a lower level and a healthy nation at a higher level and ultimately resulted in the creation of this crucial institution where people from all walks of life are welcomed to pursue their own individual lifetime dreams of excelling in sports and sports-related activities."

I don't like to fail. I don't even like to say the word. When I struggle, I want to go through the struggle and experience it fully. Only then do I find a way to overcome it. We all need to be willing to do this. It's the commitment and sacrifice I talk about. This track weighs on my heart. I believe Tanzania's Ministry of Sport wants to expand the influence of our country in the international sport community. We still have a long way to go. I believe we will get there and I still believe the future of Tanzanian athletics is at my school, but I must admit, at times this specific dream of laying down a track starts to dwindle.

At Davis's funeral, I told the attendees how much he had done to help students at my institution. It was a shame we didn't complete our work, but we did so much to be proud of. I was able to show him the pages of this book on the computer while he was in the hospital. It would be going to the printer in less than two weeks so that was as close as he got to seeing it in its final version. Coach Davis always felt strongly that an outstanding track would help us to fulfill our big dreams at Filbert Bayi Schools. I now see a track as a tribute to my mentor. Maybe when—not if—the track becomes a reality, it will be called the Ron Davis Memorial Track Facility.

I remind myself that even when it seems no one is listening, we can take small actions to move forward and invite others to get involved. Maybe the time will come where God will open the door. He has certainly done it many times before in my life. I do pray and push to find a way to see a Tartan track on the Filbert Bayi Schools campus before I die.

In 2022 at Benjamin Mkapa Stadium with Coach Ron Davis (right) at the last all-comers track and field meet he organized.

EPILOGUE

My Three Keys to Living a Legacy

On November 13, 2021, I was scheduled to take part in the Queen's Baton Relay. Much like the Olympic torch relay, it is part of the lead-up to the Commonwealth Games when it comes around every four years. That day, when the baton arrived in Dar es Salaam, it had been in 11 cities already and was on its way to dozens more around the world. It would eventually reach Birmingham, United Kingdom, for the 2022 Commonwealth Games.

Tanzania President Samia Suluhu Hassan was in attendance, and David Concar, Her Majesty's high commissioner to Tanzania, came over to the Tanzanian State House from the British Embassy to deliver a short speech for the occasion. Such presentations are formalities. I've heard thousands of them, and most of these talks are indistinguishable from all the others.

Concar's was an exception. He stepped to the podium and began:

> I wish to share a brief personal reflection about the importance of sport and the power that it has to move hearts and minds. Tanzania is indisputably a very special country. The land of Serengeti. The land of Kilimanjaro. The land of Lake Tanganyika, of Zanzibar, the Southern Highlands, all these wonderful sites and natural wonders.

> It is also the land of Julius Nyerere, one of the great architects of African independence. But before Tanzania was any of that to me personally, it was the land of Filbert Bayi.

He gestured to me in the small audience and there was applause.

> I remember I was 12 years old in 1974 when I watched Filbert Bayi triumph in the 1500 meters in the Commonwealth Games in New Zealand in what was a legendary, spellbinding, spine-tingling race where he broke the rules. He just ran out from the front and just carried on running from the front.
>
> You weren't supposed to be able to win a race like that. But he did, remarkably. That was a race that introduced me as a boy to Tanzania.

More cheers.

At the Queen's Baton Relay ceremony in Dar es Salaam with Tanzania President Samia Suluhu Hassan (center).

It made me go to my bookshelf, fetch my atlas of the world, look at the map, and ask myself, "Where is this country? Where is the land of Filbert Bayi?" And encouraged me to find out more.

So it is an enormous privilege, Madame President, to be here today more than 45 years later to share this moment with you and also with the athlete who introduced me to your country and who remains an enduring testament to the power of sport to bring people together and unlock curiosity and wonder and respect between nations.

So I want to thank you, Excellency, for being here today. I want to thank everyone else for being here to make this such a special moment for your country, for our two countries, and for the Commonwealth, and for allowing me to take this little trip down memory lane. Thank you.

So to you, Madame President, to the Queen's baton and to all those helping it on its journey across the Commonwealth, I say thank you on behalf of her Majesty the Queen, and Godspeed.

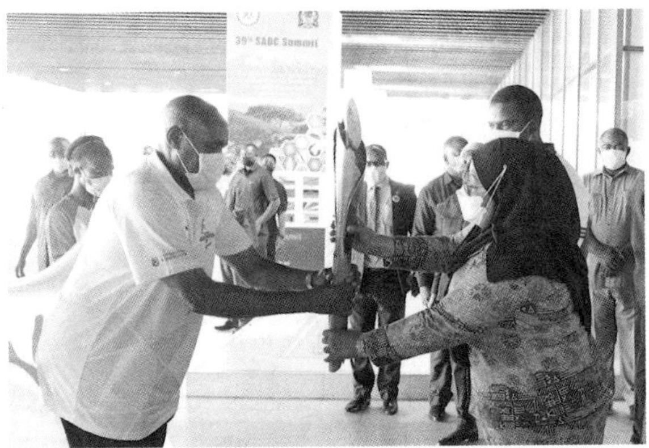

Shaking hands with President Samia Suluhu Hassan at the Queen's Baton Relay ceremony.

In those few minutes, Concar covered so much territory that I am proud to be part of. He reminded others of one of my greatest moments—what in very real ways could be called the start of my legacy—and expressed the value of "breaking rules." He reminded me that I am remembered. He showed how such memories stir our souls to curiosity and how sport can help unify countries, especially in postcolonial times.

Later, he tweeted this:

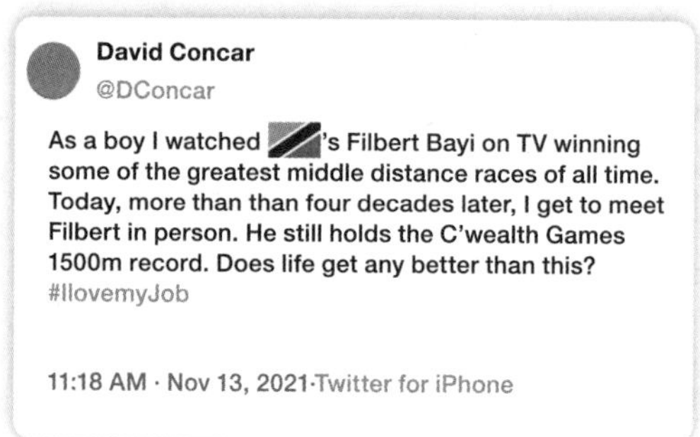

David Concar
@DConcar

As a boy I watched 's Filbert Bayi on TV winning some of the greatest middle distance races of all time. Today, more than than four decades later, I get to meet Filbert in person. He still holds the C'wealth Games 1500m record. Does life get any better than this? #IlovemyJob

11:18 AM · Nov 13, 2021·Twitter for iPhone

Going through my mind during his speech was how my willingness to work every day is perhaps my most consistent trait. I've done that throughout my entire life. That commitment to being responsible leads to a willingness to make sacrifices. Gradually, that combination develops confidence that you can accomplish whatever you set your mind to even when obstacles arise, whether it's revolutionizing racing, starting a new school, or developing a loving relationship.

Those are the three keys to living a legacy: Sacrifice. Commitment. Confidence. I hope they are an inspiration to you as you create yours, God willing, whatever it may be.

Sacrifice, commitment, and confidence are often cultivated when nobody else but God is watching. Sometimes, you don't realize that others actually are watching…peeking over your shoulder, you might say.

APPENDIXES

Appendix A

Filbert Bayi Racing Highlights

Filbert Bayi ran more than 200 high-level races in 37 countries on six continents from 1970 to 1989, including Tanzanian National Championships, East African and All-African Championships, and major international competitions around the world. Bayi ran races ranging from 800m to the marathon, on indoor and outdoor tracks, the roads, and on cross country courses.

The following list is a sampling of some of his most noteworthy performances as an elite athlete:

World records

1500m	1st	Feb. 2, 1974	Christchurch, N.Z.	3:32.16
Mile	1st	May 17, 1975	Kingston, Jamaica	3:51.0

National records

*1500m	1st	Feb. 2, 1974	Christchurch, N.Z.	3:32.16
*1500m indoor	1st	Feb. 22, 1980	San Diego, USA	3:40.3
*Mile	1st	May 17, 1975	Kingston, Jamaica	3:51.0
Mile indoor	3rd	Feb. 15, 1980	Los Angeles, USA	3:54.5
2000m	1st	Sept. 17, 1978	Schaan, Liechtenstein	4:59.21
*3000m	3rd	July 1, 1980	Oslo, Norway	7:39.27
*3000m steeple.	2nd	July 31, 1980	Moscow, Soviet Union	8:12.48

Olympic Games

3000m steeple.	dna	Sept. 1, 1972	Munich, West Germany	8:41.4
1500m	dna	Sept. 8, 1972	Munich, West Germany	3:45.4
3000m steeple.	2nd	July 31, 1980	Moscow, Soviet Union	8:12.48

Commonwealth Games

*1500m	1st	Feb. 2, 1974	Christchurch, N.Z.	3:32.16
800m	4th	Jan. 29, 1974	Christchurch, N.Z.	1:45.32
1500m	2nd	Aug. 12, 1978	Edmonton, Canada	3:35.59

All-African Games

1500m	1st	Jan. 13, 1973	Lagos, Nigeria	3:37.18
1500m	1st	July 27, 1978	Algiers, Algeria	3:36.21

**still standing*
steeple. - steeplechase
dna - did not advance

Appendix B

Men Who Held 1500m and Mile World Records Concurrently

Paavo Nurmi	FINLAND	1924-26
Jules Ladoumègue	FRANCE	1931-33
Gunder Hägg	SWEDEN	1942-43, 1945-47
Arne Andersson	SWEDEN	1943-44
John Landy	AUSTRALIA	1954-55
Herb Elliott	AUSTRALIA	1958-62
Jim Ryun	USA	1967-74
Filbert Bayi	TANZANIA	1975
Sebastian Coe	GREAT BRITAIN	1979-80
Steve Ovett	GREAT BRITAIN	1980-81
Steve Cram	GREAT BRITAIN	1985
Noureddine Morceli	ALGERIA	1993-98
Hicham El Guerrouj	MOROCCO	1999-present

REFERENCES

Bunting, Ikaweba. 1999. "The Heart of Africa." *New Internationalist*. (Jan. 1).

Butcher, Pat. 2004. "Completely Off Pace." *The Guardian*. (May 3). theguardian.com/sport/2004/may/04/athletics.comment.

Cobley, John. 2013. "Great Races #23, The 1975 Miracle Mile, Bayi v. Liquori v. Coghlan." (Jan. 30). racingpast.ca/john_contents.php?id=229.

Davies, Brett. 2022. "John Walker at 70: Here Are His 5 Finest Performances—Plus Other Highlights and His Legacy." (Jan. 12). runnerstribe.com/features/john-walker-at-70-here-are-his-5-finest-performances-plus-other-highlights-his-legacy.

Davis, Ron. 2016. "Filbert Bayi & Tanzania's Journey to First Ever Olympic Games' Medals."(Aug. 6). speedendurance.com\/2016/08/06/filbert-bayi-tanzanias-journey-to-first-ever-olympic-games-medals/).

Epstein, David. 2013. *The Sports Gene: Inside the Science of Extraordinary Athletic Performance*. New York: Penguin.

Jordan, Tom. 1975. "T&FN Interview: Filbert Bayi." *Track & Field News*. (March): 9–10.

Kidd, Bruce. 2021. *A Runner's Journey*. Toronto: University of Toronto Press.

Leivers, Carl. 2012. "Foreign Territory." *Runner's World*. (Nov. 5). runnersworld.com/advanced/a20788745/foreign-territory/.

Liquori, Marty, and Skip Myslenski. 1979. *On the Run: In Search of the Perfect Race*. New York: William Morrow.

MacDonald, Hugh. 2014. "Bayi's Record May Be Gone But It Should Never Be Forgotten." *Glasgow Herald*. (Jan. 29). heraldscotland.com/sport/13143168.bayis-record-may-gone-never-forgotten/.

New Zealand Herald. 2014. "In Their Words: The Race That Stopped a Nation." (Jan. 30). nzherald.co.nz/sport/in-their-words-the-race-that-stopped-a-nation/KHAHYR32DNE73AYGRD46UJ43GI.

Perovich, Kathy. 1982. "At 29, Stellar Runner Bayi to Become OU Freshman." *Daily Oklahoman*. (Sept. 15). oklahoman.com/article/1996088/at-29-stellar-runner-bayi-to-become-ou-freshman.

Prokop, Dave, ed. 1975. *The African Running Revolution*. Mountain View, Calif.: World Publications.

Reid, Ron. 1975. "The Quickening Education of Filbert Bayi." *Sports Illustrated*. (May 26). vault.si.com/vault/1975/05/26/a-record-goes-bust.

Riga, Andy. 2016. "Montreal Olympics: African Boycott of 1976 Games 'Changed the World.'" *Montreal Gazette*. (July 19). montrealgazette.com/sports/montreal-olympics-african-boycott-of-1976-games-changed-the-world.

Rowbottom, Mike. 2019. "Bayi Recounts Legendary 1974 1500m World Record Run." World Athletics. (Dec. 21). worldathletics.org/news/news/mile-legends-reunion-iaaf-heritage.

Schrag, Myles. 2019. "Ron Davis and Filbert Bayi: Looking to Past for its Athletic Future, Part 2." (Feb. 13). speedendurance.com/2019/02/13/ron-davis-filbert-bayi-looking-to-past-for-its-athletics-future-part-2.

Smith, Gary. 1994. "An Exclusive Club." *Sports Illustrated*. (June 27). vault.si.com/vault/1994/06/27/an-exclusive-club-forty-years-after-roger-bannister-broke-four-minutes-the-brotherhood-of-mile-record-holders-gathered-to-honor-their-grand-obsession.

Tuluwami, Haile. 2011. "Filbert Bayi, the Boldest Runner Ever." (May 4). moti-athletics-histo.blogspot.com/2011/05/filbert-bayi-bravest-runner-ever.html.

PHOTO AND ILLUSTRATION CREDITS

Front cover—Ed Lacey/Popperfoto via Getty Images.

Part One—Page 1: Courtesy Filbert Bayi and family.

Chapter 1—Page 4: Map by Dariusz Janczewski; page 6: Courtesy Filbert Bayi and family.

Chapter 2—Page 11: Map by Dariusz Janczewski.

Chapter 4—Pages 28 and 32: Courtesy Filbert Bayi and family.

Part Two—Page 35: Tony Duffy/Getty Images.

Chapter 5—Page 39: Ed Lacey/Popperfoto via Getty Images; page 41: IMAGO/Sven Simon.

Chapter 7—Page 59: Tony Duffy/Allsport via Getty Images; page 60: Ed Lacey/Popperfoto via Getty Images; page 63: Courtesy *Track & Field News*; pages 66 and 68: Courtesy Filbert Bayi and family.

Chapter 8—Page 70: Stuff Limited.

Chapter 9—Page 82: Courtesy *Track & Field News*.

Chapter 10—Page 86: Map by Dariusz Janczewski.

Chapter 11—Page 97: Courtesy *Track & Field News*; page 100: Heinz Kluetmeier/*Sports Illustrated* via Getty Images; page 102: (race) IMAGO/ZUMA Wire; (trophy) Aubrey Hart/Evening Standard/Getty Images.

Chapter 12—Page 106: Courtesy *Track & Field News*; page 108: George Long/*Sports Illustrated* via Getty Images; page 113: Courtesy Suleiman Nyambui.

Chapter 13—Page 117: Courtesy Filbert Bayi and family; page 118: Courtesy Filbert Bayi and family; page 120: S&G/PA Images via Getty Images; page 122: Bob Thomas Sports Photography via Getty Images.

Chapter 14—Page 129: IMAGO/Sven Simon.

Chapter 15—Page 135: John Patrick O'Gready/Fairfax Media via Getty Images.

Chapter 16—Page 148: IMAGO/Werner Schulze; page 151: Bob Thomas Sports Photography via Getty Images; page 153: Photo George Herringshaw.

Part Three—Page 155: Courtesy Myles Schrag.

Chapter 17—Pages 166 and 168: Courtesy Filbert Bayi and family.

Chapter 18—Pages 176: Courtesy Filbert Bayi and family; pages 177 and 179: Courtesy Myles Schrag; page 180: Courtesy Filbert Bayi and family; page 182: Courtesy Myles Schrag.

Chapter 19—Page 184: (street sign, wall drawings, and bus) Courtesy Myles Schrag; (students) Courtesy Filbert Bayi and family; pages 188–9: Michael Stephens - PA Images/PA Images via Getty Images; page 191: Bob Martin/*Sports Illustrated* via Getty Images/Getty Images; page 192: John Lukuwi/AFP via Getty Images; page 194: (both photos) Courtesy Filbert Bayi and family; Page 196: Courtesy Dariusz Janczewski; Page 198: IMAGO/Xinhua.

Chapter 20—Pages 200–2, 204, 206–8: (all nine photos) Courtesy Filbert Bayi and family.

Chapter 21—Page 211: World Athletics Heritage; page 212: (both photos) World Athletics Heritage; page 213: World Athletics Heritage; pages 214 (Anna and Keino) and 217: Courtesy Filbert Bayi and family; page 218: Courtesy Wayne Angel; page 220: (both photos) Courtesy Filbert Bayi and family; page 222: Courtesy Henry Benny Tandau.

Epilogue — Pages 224–6: Courtesy Tanzania State House.

ACKNOWLEDGMENTS

I BELIEVE IN THE IMPORTANCE OF CONFIDENCE, SACRIFICE, AND commitment in reaching goals and living with purpose. Those same attributes are needed to create a book, and I am blessed to have many people help me tell my life story. It's the only way you can now hold this book in your hands.

While I wish to thank some people here, it is the "curse" of having lived such a blessed life that I will surely leave out some who also deserve to be included. I hope anybody in that category will forgive me in advance.

Most importantly, I wish to thank my family. That includes my mother, who instilled a strong work ethic and courage in me at a young age, and my father, whom I never met but lives inside me. It also includes my dearly departed wife, Anna, our four children (Engelbert, Annette, Harriette, and Cuthbert), and our school family—the staff of Filbert Bayi Schools (FBS) and Foundation (FBF) who always go the extra mile to keep things moving when I'm occupied with other duties.

I was honored to serve with my fellow soldiers in the Air Wing Barracks of the Tanzanian Army. They made up my military family for more than 30 years. In particular, Major General Mrisho Hagai Sarakikya, retired Chief of Defense Forces (CDF), inspired and encouraged me and contributed a lot to my athletic and military performance and success.

Also, the late Chediel Mgonja, former Tanzanian Minister of Sport, worked with the German ambassador to allow me to get treatment for malaria at the tropical diseases hospital in Hamburg in the late 1970s. This effort gave me the opportunity to achieve my Olympic dream.

Coach Ron Davis, my former coach, will always be part of my family. He unfortunately passed away just before we completed this book. But he is the reason it came to be. Ron introduced me to Myles Schrag and Soulstice Publishing, a team that has worked hard to make the book a reality and partnered with Meyer & Meyer to ensure the book is available worldwide. In the truest sense, this book would not have happened without Ron's encouragement, belief, and determination.

Alice Annibali and staff at World Athletics, from President Lord Sebastian Coe on down, have been amazing supporters of this project throughout. Dame Louise Martin, president of the Commonwealth Games Federation, and her staff have been equally supportive, as has Madame Miriam, president of the African Region for the Commonwealth Games, and the Association of African National Olympic Committees (ANOCA). They care deeply about the legacy of our sport.

I'm grateful to rightsholders of photographs who made it possible to include many images in the book. Since my biggest athletic moments were more than 40 years ago now, it means a lot to me that readers can catch a glimpse of those days. This list includes Cathy Rincón-Mergenthaler, Imago Stock & People; Neil Loft, Getty Images; Garry Hill, Track & Field News; Jude Tewnion, Stuff Ltd.; and George Herringshaw, Sporting-Heroes.net.

Much gratitude as well to friends and competitors who helped jog my memory about details from decades ago and Jeff Benjamin for helping me connect to some of them. This group includes Rod Dixon, Marty Liquori, Craig Masback, Suleiman Nyambui, and Helen and John Walker. As I say throughout the book, these men brought out the best in me and helped make it possible for me to live my best life.

As I'm sure you noticed, I'm proud of my country and want to thank our sixth President of the United Republic of Tanzania, the Honorable Samia Suluhu Hassan, for her vision in sports development. Also, thanks to the Tanzanian National Olympic Committee, including President Mr. Gulam Abdulla Rashid, Vice President Mr. Henry Benny Tandau,

Assistant General Secretary Mr. Suleiman Moh'd Jabir, all other executive board members and staff, and the presidents and secretaries general of the national sport associations and federations of the Tanzanian mainland and Zanzibar.

When British High Commissioner, His Excellency David Concar, spoke at the Tanzania State House during the Queen's Baton Relay celebration, he spoke eloquently about why Tanzania has much to take pride in. I want to thank him for sharing his memories that day, expressing kind words about "the country of Filbert Bayi," and without knowing it, providing ideal material for the epilogue of this book.

Segun Odegbami, never afraid of hyperbole, said inspiring words in his foreword, calling me "a humble pilgrim, singular athlete, pride of Africa, and a god of the track." Segun was a fine athlete in his own right as a Nigerian footballer, and now he is a passionate voice for sport in the service of development and diplomacy. Africa and the world are fortunate to have him in this role, seeing the best in sport and providing a platform for it to live up to that potential.

Finally, I thank fans of distance running who haven't forgotten our sport's rich history. I encourage them to pass on their interest to the younger generations. I have done my best to capture some of those moments in this book and am humbled to have played a part in them. If I remembered any events inaccurately and there are any mistakes, they are mine alone.

ABOUT THE AUTHORS

Filbert Bayi's legacy in middle-distance running is assured as his blistering pace energized the sport in the 1970s, leading to his becoming the first Black man to hold the mile and 1500m world records. He earned the first Olympic medal ever for Tanzania with his silver medal in the 3000m steeplechase at the 1980 Olympics. With his wife, Anna, he established Filbert Bayi Schools and the Filbert Bayi Foundation in Kibaha, Tanzania, which for more than 20 years has represented excellence by educating thousands of students and creating an even larger legacy off the track.

Myles Schrag is co-founder of Soulstice Publishing and author of eight books. He holds a master's degree in kinesiology from University of Illinois at Urbana-Champaign and has helped more than 200 books reach publication as either an acquisitions editor, developmental editor, publisher, or manuscript broker.

ABOUT THE PUBLISHER

Soulstice Publishing brings to life "books with soul" that inspire readers with stories of human potential realized and celebrate our unique position in the Southwest.

Soulstice took root in our mountain town of Flagstaff, Arizona, which sits at the base of the San Francisco Peaks, on homelands sacred to Native Americans throughout the region. We honor their past, present, and future generations, as well as their original and ongoing care for the lands we also hold dear.

Surrounded by ponderosa pines, enriched by diverse cultures, and inspired by the optimistic Western spirit, Flagstaff abounds with scientists, artists, athletes, and many other people who love the outdoors. It is quite an inspiring place to live. Considering the dearth of oxygen at our 7,000-foot elevation, you might say it leaves us breathless.

Learn more at **soulsticepublishing.com**
Soulstice Publishing, LLC

PO Box 791
Flagstaff, AZ 86002
(928) 814-8943
connect@soulsticepublishing.com